ESSENTIAL

Contract Law

Titles in the series:

ESSENTIAL

Contract Law

by

Marnah Suff, BA, LLB, Cert F Ed, Barrister
Senior Lecturer in Law
Swansea Law School

First published in Great Britain 1994 by Cavendish Publishing
Limited, The Glass House, Wharton Street, London WC1X 9PX

Telephone: 0171-278 8000   Facsimile: 0171-278 8080

British Library Cataloguing in Publication Data

Suff, Marnah
Essential Contract Law –
(Essential Law Series)
I Title II Series
344.2062

ISBN 1-85941-122-3
Printed and bound in Great Britain

Foreword

This book is part of the Cavendish Essential series. The books in the series are designed to provide useful revision aids for the hard-pressed student. They are not, of course, intended to be substitutes for more detailed treatises. Other textbooks in the Cavendish portfolio must supply these gaps.

Each book in the series follows a uniform format of a checklist of the areas covered in each chapter, expanded treatment of 'Essential' issues looking at examination topics in depth, followed by 'Revision Notes' for self-assessment.

The team of authors bring a wealth of lecturing and examining experience to the task in hand. Many of us can even recall what it was like to face law examinations!

Professor Nicholas Bourne
General Editor, Essential Series
Swansea Law School

Summer 1994

Preface

This book is intended as a revision aid for students studying for degree or professional examinations in the law of contract. As space is limited, the book concentrates on those areas of the law which are found in most contract syllabi, including that of the External LLB of the University of London. Topics not covered include the history of the law of contract, form, gaming and wagering contracts, agency, assignment, and quasi-contracts.

The law is stated as it was on the first of May 1994.

My thanks are due to Mrs Maureen Turner, wihout whose advice and assistance this book would not have been possible.

Marnah Suff

Table of contents

1 Agreement

The need for a valid offer and a valid acceptance

The fact that an agreement has been reached will often be obvious. The terms will have been set out in a written agreement signed by both parties. However, where the agreement has been reached orally, or by conduct, there can be problems and in such cases, the dealings between the parties are traditionally analysed in terms of offer and acceptance. Has there been a valid offer made by one party, and a valid acceptance of that offer by the other party?

Lord Denning suggested a more flexible approach in *Gibson v Manchester City Council* (1978). In this case the local authority wrote to Mr Gibson stating the council 'may be prepared to sell the house to you at the purchase price of £2,725 less 20% = £2,180' and enclosing an application form. Mr Gibson returned the completed application form on the 5 March, and wrote again on the 18 March requesting the council to carry on with the purchase. Before contracts could be exchanged, the political control of the council changed, and they discontinued the policy of selling council houses. Mr Gibson sued to enforce his agreement with the council. Lord Denning stated that there was no need for a formal offer and acceptance. He suggested that if from the correspondence it was clear that the parties were agreed on all material terms, then there was a binding contract even though the formalities had not been gone through. He reiterated that view in *Butler Machine Tool Co Ltd v Excello Corp Ltd* (1979)(see below).

conduct of parties

However, the traditional need for offer and acceptance was re-stressed by the House of Lords in *Gibson v Manchester Council* (1979). Lord Diplock stated that the need for an offer and an acceptance would only be dispensed with in rare atypical cases eg in *Clarke v Dunraven* (1897) where the entrants in a race were not in direct contact with each other, but were in contact with the organisers of the race. It was held that there was a contract between two individual competitors.

Lord Wilberforce expressed some dissatisfaction with the need to force facts to 'fit uneasily into the marked slots of offer, acceptance and consideration' in *The Eurymedon* (below) and the argument has again been revived by Lord Justice Steyn who declared in *Trentham Ltd v Archital Luxfer* (1993) that a strict analysis of offer and acceptance was not necessary in cases where there was an executed contract in a commercial setting (in that case a building contract).

However, until the House of Lords declares otherwise, it seems that an identification of a valid offer and a valid acceptance of that offer is still necessary in normal circumstances.

Unilateral and bilateral agreements

A bilateral contract consists of an exchange of promises. A 'bilateral' offer, therefore, seeks a *promise* in return, eg Offer – 'I will sell you my car for £500.' Acceptance – 'I will pay £500 for your car.'

In a unilateral contract only one party makes a promise, ie the offeror, 'I will pay £500 to anyone who will find my lost kitten and return it to me.' Acceptance occurs when the lost kitten is returned. A 'unilateral' offer is accepted by doing what is requested in the offer. The offeree does not enter into any promises: he either fulfils the condition or he does not, eg *Carlill v Carbolic Smoke Ball Co* (see below).

The distinction between bilateral and unilateral contracts is important with regard to:

- advertisements;
- revocation of offers;
- communication of acceptance.

Identification of a valid offer

Definition

A promise to be bound to certain terms if the other party responds.
A valid offer:

- Must be communicated, so that the other party may accept or reject it. In *Taylor v Laird* (1856) the master of a ship gave up his command during a voyage, but helped to sail the ship home. It was held that the owners did not have to pay for his assistance; an offer to assist had not been communicated to them, so they had not had an opportunity to accept or reject.
- May be communicated in any manner whatsoever, ie in writing, in words, or by conduct. There is no general requirement that an agreement must be in writing. *except in contract for Sale of Land*
- May be made to a particular person, to a group of persons, or to the whole world. In *Carlill v Carbolic Smoke Ball Company* (1893) the defendants, who manufactured 'carbolic smoke balls', issued an advertisement in which they offered to pay £100 to any person who used one of their smoke balls and then succumbed to influenza within a specified time. Mrs Carlill, after seeing the advertisement, bought and used the smoke ball and promptly went down with influenza. She sued the defendants for the £100. The defendants argued, *inter alia*, that an offer to the 'whole world' was not possible in English law. It was held that an offer *can* be made to the 'whole world'.
- Must be definite in substance (see certainty of terms and incomplete agreements below).
- Must be distinguished from an 'invitation to treat'.

Invitations to treat

An invitation to treat is an indication that the invitor is willing to enter into negotiations but is not yet prepared to be bound, eg in *Gibson v Manchester City Council* (1979) the council's letter stated 'we may be prepared to sell you'. A response to an invitation to treat does not lead to an agreement; the response itself may be an offer.

The distinction between an offer and an invitation to treat depends on the intention of the parties, and this must be judged objectively.

The courts have already established that there is no intention to be bound in the following cases.

Display of goods for sale

- In a shop
  In *Pharmaceutical Society of GB v Boots Ltd* (1953) the Court of Appeal held that in a self-service shop, the sale takes place at the check out counter, when the assistant accepts the customer's offer to buy the goods. The goods on the shelves are mere invitations to treat, ie an invitation to the customer to make an offer for the goods.
- In a shop window
  In *Fisher v Bell* (1961) it was held that a 'flick knife' displayed in a shop window with a price attached was an invitation to treat.
- In an advertisement
  In *Partridge v Crittenden* (1968) an advertisement which said 'bramblefinch cocks and hens - 25s' was held to be an invitation to treat. The court pointed out that if the advertisement was treated as an offer this could lead to many actions for breach of contract against the advertiser, since his stock of birds was limited and, therefore, he could not have intended the advertisement to be an offer.

However, if the advertisement is unilateral in nature, then the advertisement will be an offer. In *Lefkowitz v Great Minneapolis Stores* (1957) the advertisement stated 'Saturday 9 am sharp. Three brand new fur coats worth £100. First come first served. £1 each.' The US court held that this was a unilateral offer. See also *Carlill v Carbolic Smoke Ball Co Ltd* (above). An advertisement of a reward may also be a unilateral offer.

Auctions

- An auctioneer's request for bids
  In *Payne v Cave* (1789) it was held that the auctioneer's request was an invitation to treat. The offer was made by the bidder.
- A notice of an auction
  In *Harris v Nickerson* (1873) it was held that a notice that an auction would be held on a certain date was not an offer which could be accepted by turning up at the stated time.

If the auction is stated to be 'without reserve' then there is still no necessity to hold an auction. However, if the auction is held, it must be 'without reserve' (*Warlow v Harrison* (1859)).

Tenders

A request for tenders is normally an invitation to treat.

However, it was held in *Harvela Ltd v Royal Trust of Canada* (1985) that if the request is made to specified parties and it is stated that the contract will be awarded to the lowest or the highest bidder, then this will be binding as a unilateral offer. It was also held that a referential bid, eg the highest other bid plus 10% 'was not a valid bid'. It was held in *Blackpool and Fylde Aero Club v Blackpool BC* (1990) that if the request is addressed to specified parties, this amounts to a unilateral offer that serious consideration will be given to each tender.

'Subject to contract'
The words 'subject to contract' may be placed on top of a letter in order to indicate that certain statements are not to be to be legally binding (*Walford v Miles* (1992)).

Sale of land
In negotiations for the sale of land the court will examine the wording used particularly carefully. In *Harvey v Facey* (1893) the plaintiffs telegraphed the defendants, 'Will you sell Bumper Hall Pen? Telegraph lowest price for Bumper Hall Pen.' The defendants replied, 'Lowest price for Bumper Hall Pen £900.' It was held that this was supplying information (ie an invitation to treat), not an offer.

Timetables and buses
There is no clear authority on offers and invitations to treat in the case of passenger bus services. It was suggested by Lord Greene in *Wilkie v London Transport Board* (1947) that the offer was made by the bus company, and it was accepted by the passenger when he boarded the bus.

Termination of the offer

An offer may be terminated in one of three ways.

Revocation (termination by the offeror)
- An offeror may withdraw an offer at any time before it has been accepted.
- The revocation must be communicated to the offeree before acceptance. In *Byrne v Van Tienhoven* (1880) the withdrawal of an offer sent by telegram was held to be communicated only when the telegram was received.

It has been held that communication need not be made by the offeree; communication through a third party will suffice. In *Dickenson v Dodds* (1876) the plaintiff, to whom the defendant had offered to sell a farm for £800, was told by a neighbour that the farm had been sold to a third party. He then purported to accept the offer. It was held that at the time of 'acceptance' he was aware that the offer had been validly revoked. (This decision has been criticised by both Treitel and Anson as it creates problems for the offeree who must adjudge the reliability of the third party and his information.)

* An offer to keep an offer open for a certain length of time can be withdrawn like any other, unless an option has been purchased (ie consideration has been given to keep the offer open).
* There are special problems attached to the revocation of unilateral offers.

Communication of the revocation is difficult if the offer was to the whole world. It was suggested, however, in the American case of *Shuey v USA* (1875) that communication will be assumed if the offeror takes reasonable steps to inform the public, ie places an advertisement in the same newspaper.

It now seems established that revocation cannot take place if the offeree has started to perform, eg she has been promised £500 if she walks from London to York. If she has started the journey, she must be given an opportunity to complete her performance. In *Errington v Errington* (1952) a father promised his daughter and son-in-law that if they paid off the mortgage on a house he owned, he would give it to them. The young couple duly paid the instalments, but the father withdrew his offer shortly before the whole debt was paid. It was held that there was an implied term that the offer was irrevocable once performance had begun. This is also supported by dicta in *Daulia v Four Milbank Nominees* (1978).

Lapse (termination by operation of law)

An offer may lapse and thus cannot be accepted because of:
* Passage of time, either
(a) at the end of a stipulated time (if any); or
(b) if no time is stipulated, after a reasonable time. In *Ramsgate Victoria Hotel Co v Montefiore* (1866) an attempt to accept an offer to buy shares after five months failed since the offer had clearly lapsed.
* Death
(a) of the offeror if the offer was of a personal nature;
(b) of the offeree.

- Failure of a condition, either
(a) an express condition; or
(b) an implied condition. In *Financings Ltd v Stimpson* (1962) it was held by the court that an offer to buy a car lapsed when the car was badly damaged on the ground that the offer contained an implied term that the car would remain in the condition it was in when the offer was made.

Rejection (termination by the offeree)

Counter-offer

Traditionally, an acceptance must be a mirror image of the offer. If any alteration is made, or anything added, then this will be a counter-offer, and will terminate the offer. In *Hyde v Wrench* (1840) the defendant offered to sell a farm for £1,000. The plaintiff said he would give £950 for it. The court held that this was a counter-offer which terminated the original offer which was, therefore, no longer open for acceptance. In *Brogden v Metropolitan Rly Co* (1877) the defendant sent a written agreement which had been negotiated to the plaintiff for signature. The plaintiff signed the agreement and entered the name of an arbitrator in a space which had been left empty for this purpose. It was held that the returned document was not an acceptance but a counter-offer.

This is particularly important for businesses who contract by means of sales forms and purchase forms, eg if an order placed by the seller's purchase form is 'accepted' on the seller's sales' form, and the conditions on the back of the two forms are not identical (which they are very unlikely to be) then the 'acceptance' is a counter-offer, ie an implied rejection. In *Butler Machine Tool Co Ltd v Excello Corporation Ltd* (1979) the sellers offered to sell a machine tool to the buyers for £75,535 on their own conditions of sale which were stated to prevail over any conditions in the buyer's order form, and which contained a price variation clause. The buyers 'accepted' the offer on their own order form which stated that the price was a fixed price, and which contained a tear off slip which said 'We accept your order on the terms and conditions stated thereon.' The sellers signed and returned the slip together with a letter which stated that they were carrying out the order in accordance with their original offer. When they delivered the machine they claimed the price had increased by £2,892. The buyers refused to pay the extra sum. It was held that the contract was concluded on the buyer's terms; the signing and returning of the tear-off slip was conclusive. The majority analysed the transaction by applying the 'mirror image' rules, but Lord Denning argued that the traditional rules were out of date, and that a better approach would be to look at the documents to see whether agreement has been reached on all material points, even though there may be differences on the back of the printed forms (*cf Gibson* above). The majority of the Court of Appeal, however, applied the traditional rules.

Note

A request for further information is not a counter-offer. In *Stevenson v McClean* (1880) the defendant offered to sell iron to the plaintiff at 40s a ton. The plaintiff telegraphed to enquire whether he could pay by instalments. It was held that this was a mere enquiry for information, not a counter-offer.

Conditional or qualified acceptance

A conditional acceptance may be a counter-offer capable of acceptance, eg 'I will pay £500 for your car if you paint it red'; or it may be qualified acceptance as in the phrase, 'subject to contract'.

Identification of a valid acceptance

An acceptance is a final and unqualified assent to all the terms of the offer.

- It must be made while the offer is still in force. (See termination of offer above.)
- It must be made by the offeree.
- It must exactly match the terms of the offer ie it must be a 'mirror image' of the offer (see counter-offers above).
- It may be written, oral, or implied from conduct. In *Brogden v Metropolitan Rly* (1877) (above) the returned document was held to be a counter-offer which the defendants then accepted either by ordering coal from Brogden or by accepting delivery of the coal. (See also *Butler MTC v Excello Corp*, above.)

However, the offeror may require the acceptance to be made in a certain way. If the requirement is mandatory, it must be followed. If the requirement is directory, then another equally effective method will suffice. In *Manchester Diocesan Council for Education v Commercial and General Investments Ltd* (1969) an invitation to tender stated that the person whose bid was accepted would be informed by a letter to the address given in the tender. The acceptance was eventually sent not to this address, but to the defendant's surveyor. It was held that the statement in the tender was not mandatory; the tender had therefore been validly accepted.

- Where the offer is made in alternative terms, the acceptance must make it clear to which set of terms it relates.
- A person cannot accept an offer of which he has no knowledge. In *R v Clarke* (1927) (Australia) it was held that Clarke could not claim a reward which had been offered for information he had given because at the time he gave the information the reward was not in his mind. The court stated, 'there cannot be assent without knowledge of the offer'. But a person's motive in accepting the offer is irrelevant. In *Williams v Cawardine* (1833) (Australia) the plaintiff was held entitled to a reward for information given mainly in order to salve her conscience. She was aware of the offer, however, when she gave the information, and the court stated, 'we cannot go into the plaintiff's motives'.
- 'Cross-offers' do not constitute an agreement (*Tinn v Hoffman & Co* (1873)).

Acceptance must be communicated

Acceptance must be communicated by the offeror or his agent. In *Powell v Lee* (1908) an unauthorised communication by one of the managers that the Board of Managers had selected a particular candidate for a headship was held not a valid acceptance.

Silence as communication

An offeror may not stipulate that the silence of the offeree will amount to an acceptance. In *Felthouse v Bindley* (1862) the plaintiff wrote to his nephew offering to buy a horse, and adding, 'If I hear no more ... I will take it that the horse is mine.' The nephew did not reply to this letter, but told the defendant, an auctioneer who was to sell his stock, that this horse was to be kept out of the sale. It was held there was no contract. Acceptance had not been communicated to the offeror.

It has been suggested that this does not mean that silence can *never* amount to acceptance, eg if in *Felthouse v Bindley* the offeree had relied on the offeror's statement that he need not communicate his acceptance, the court could interpret that the need for acceptance had been waived by the offeror (see below).

In *The Hannah Blumenthal* (1983) the House of Lords held that a contract to abandon a reference to arbitration could be concluded by the prolonged silence of both parties, but this is a rare example of silence amounting to acceptance.

Exceptions to the rule that acceptance must be communicated

* Where communication is expressly (see above *Felthouse v Bindley*) or impliedly (see *Carlill v Carbolic Smoke Ball Co*) waived.
* Where failure of communication is the fault of the offeror. This was suggested by Lord Denning in *Entores Ltd v Miles Far East Corporation* (1955) where he stated, 'if the listener on the telephone does not catch the words of acceptance, but nevertheless does not ask for them to be repeated, or if the acceptance is sent by telex during business hours but is simply not read by anyone in the offeror's office when it is there transcribed on his machine'.
* Where the post is deemed to be the proper method of communication. In *Adams v Linsell* (1818) the defendants wrote to the plaintiffs offering to sell them a quantity of wool and requiring acceptance by post. The letter arrived late, having been incorrectly addressed by the defendants. The plaintiffs immediately posted an acceptance on 5 December. It was held that the contract was completed on 5 December.

The postal rule

Acceptance takes place when a letter is posted, not when it is received. (see *Adams v Linsell* (1818)).

Acceptance is effective on posting, even when the letter is lost in the post. In *Household Fire Insurance Co Ltd v Grant* (1879) the defendant offered to buy shares in the plaintiff's company. A letter of allotment was posted to the defendant but it never reached him. It was held that the contract was completed when the letter was posted.

Note
The interplay between acceptance and revocation by post. In *Byrne v Van-Tienhoven* (1880) the defendants posted a letter in Cardiff on 1 October offering to sell 1,000 boxes of tinplate to the plaintiffs in New York. On 8 October they posted a letter revoking the offer. The plaintiffs posted a letter accepting the original offer on the 15 October. Under the postal rules of acceptance, acceptance took place when the letter was posted. Revocation, however, did not take place until the letter was actually received on 20 October, by which time the contract had been formed.

Limitation of the rule

Limitations of the postal rule are such that:

- it only applies to letters and telegrams;
- it does not apply to methods of instantaneous communication;
- it must be reasonable to use the post as the means of communication (eg an offer by telephone or by fax might indicate that a rapid method of response was required);
- letters of acceptance must be properly addressed and stamped;
- the rule is easily displaced eg it may be excluded by the offeror either expressly or impliedly. In *Holwell Securities Ltd v Hughes* (1974) it was excluded by the offeror requiring 'notice in writing'. It was also suggested by the court that the rule would not be used where it would lead to manifest inconvenience.

Query

Can a letter of acceptance be cancelled by *actual* communication before the letter is delivered? There is no direct English authority on this point.

Arguments against

- Once a letter is posted the offer is accepted; there is no provision in law for revoking an acceptance.
- It was not accepted in the New Zealand Case of *Wenkeim v Arndt* (1873) nor in the South African case of *A to Z Bazaars (Pty) Ltd v Minister of Agriculture* (1974).
- Cheshire argues that it would be unfair to the offeror who would be bound as soon as the letter was posted, but would allow the offeree to keep his options open.

Arguments for

- It was allowed in the Scottish case of *Countess of Dunmore v Alexander* (1830).
- It is argued that actual prior communication of rejection would not necessarily prejudice the offeror. Treitel sees no reason why a rule setting out the relationship between revocation and acceptance and what happens when a letter is lost in the post should also govern cancellation of an acceptance by post.
- It is also argued that it would be absurd to insist on enforcing a contract when both parties had acted on the recall – this could be interpreted as an agreement to discharge.

Communication by instantaneous/electronic means

Acceptance takes place when and where the message is received.

The rules on telephones and telex were laid down in *Entores v Miles* (above) and confirmed in *Brinkibon Ltd v Stalag Stahl* (1983) where it was held that during normal office hours, acceptance takes place when the message is printed out, not when it is read. The House of Lords, however, accepted that communication by Telex may not always be instantaneous, eg when received at night or when the office was closed. Lord Wilberforce stated 'No universal rule could cover all such cases; they must be resolved by reference to the intention of the parties, by sound business practice and, in some cases, by a judgment of where the risk should lie'. It has been suggested that a message sent outside business hours should be 'communicated' when it is expected that it would be read, ie at the next opening of business. It is generally accepted that the same rules should relate to faxes and to telex.

There is no direct authority on telephone answering machines. On the one hand it is argued that the presence of an answering machine indicates that communication is not instantaneous; there is a delay between sending and receiving messages. The offeror has set the answering machine and, therefore, any risk should lie with him, thus, the postal rule should apply. On the other hand, it is argued that the postal rule is itself controversial and is unlikely to be extended. It has been suggested that until the matter is dealt with by the court, the basic rule should apply, ie that acceptance must be communicated. Acceptance, therefore, takes place when the message is actually heard by the offeror.

Certainty of terms and incomplete agreements

It is for the parties to make their intentions clear. If an agreement is too vague, the courts will not enforce it. In *Scammell & Nephew v Ouston* (1941) the courts refused to enforce a sale stated to be made 'on hire-purchase terms'; neither the rate of interest, not the period of repayment, nor the number of instalments were stated.

An agreement to agree in the future, ie an agreement to make an agreement, will not constitute a binding contract. In *Walford v Miles* (1992) an agreement to negotiate in good faith was held to be too vague, but it was stated that a 'lock-out agreement', ie an agreement not to negotiate with anyone else is valid provided it is clearly stated and for a specific length of time. This was applied by the Court of Appeal in *Pitt v PHH Asset Management* (1993) where a promise not to negotiate with any third party for two weeks was enforced.

In *May & Butcher v R* (1934) it was held that an agreement to buy petrol 'at a price to be agreed between the parties' was void as an incomplete agreement.

But the uncertainty may be cured by:

- A trade custom, where a word has a specific meaning.
- Previous dealings between the parties whereby a word or phrase has acquired a specific meaning, eg timber of 'fair specification' in *Hillas v Arcos* (1932).
- The contract itself, which provides a method for resolving an uncertainty. In *Foley v Classique Coaches* (1934) there was an *executed* contract where the vagueness of 'at a price to be agreed' was cured by a provision in the contract referring disputes to arbitration, cf *May & Butcher v R*, an *unexecuted* contract, where the court refused to allow a similar arbitration clause to cure the uncertainty.

The courts will strive to find a contract valid where it has been executed.

The Sale of Goods Act 1979 provides that if no price or mechanism for fixing the price is provided, then the buyer must pay a 'reasonable price', but this provision will not apply where the contract states that the price is 'to be agreed between the parties'.

Application of all above rules to tenders

- Requests for tenders are invitations to treat. But if it is made to specific persons and states that 'lowest' or 'highest' bid will be accepted, then it is an offer (see above). If it is made to specific persons, there is also an implied term that the tender will be considered.
- If the tender is 'to supply goods as and when required', then it is an incomplete agreement; acceptance of such a tender does not create a contract. The tender amounts to a standing offer. Each order will amount to an acceptance and will constitute a separate contract. The offeror may revoke the offer in between orders, and the offeree need not place any orders at all.
- If the tender is to supply goods as 'sole supplier' the tenderer may not insist on any goods being ordered, but if goods of that description are ordered, it must be from the tenderer.

Objective nature of test for agreement

The court adopts an objective, rather than a subjective, approach in deciding whether an agreement has been reached. It places a reasonable interpretation on the behaviour of the parties, rather than seeking a *consensus ad idem* (a meeting of minds).

Situations where the courts have found a contract without a *consensus ad idem* are:

- Under the postal rule, when the offeree may have tried to revoke the acceptance before the offeror reads the letter of acceptance.

  In *Butler v Excello Corp* (above) the seller did not consider that he had accepted the buyers' terms.

- Where there is a mutual mistake or unilateral mistake which does not amount to an operative mistake as in *Smith v Hughes* (see Chapter 5).

Conversely there are cases where there is *consensus ad idem* but no contract:

- Contracts which must be made in writing.
- Agreements which lack capacity.
- Cases where the parties seem to be agreed on all material issues, but there is no technical offer and acceptance (*Gibson v Manchester City Council* (above) *Felthouse v Bindley* (above)).

Revision Notes

Agreement is reached by valid offer and valid acceptance

However, a more flexible approach was suggested by:
- Lord Denning in *Gibson v Manchester City Council* (1978) and *Butler Machine Tool Co Ltd v Excello Corp Ltd* (1979).
- Lord Justice Steyn in *Trentham Ltd v Archital Luxfer* (1993).

Both considered that a strict application of the rules of offer and acceptance was not necessary.

However, the traditional rules were applied by the House of Lords in *Gibson v Manchester City Council* (1979).

An offer is a promise to be bound to certain terms if the other party responds

A valid offer must be communicated orally, in writing or by conduct. It may be open, ie to anyone who wishes to accept (*Carlill v Carbolic Smoke Ball Company* (1893)). It must be definite in substance, and distinguished from an 'invitation to treat', ie a commencement of negotiation.

Examples of invitations to treat

Display of goods for sale
Pharmaceutical Society of GB v Boots Ltd (1953)
Fisher v Bell (1961)

Advertisements
Partridge v Crittenden (1968)
However, if the advertisement is unilateral in nature, then the advertisement will be an offer:
Carlill v Carbolic Smoke Ball Co Ltd (1893)
Lefkowitz v Great Minneapolis Surplus Stores (1957).
Reward cases

Auctions
Payne v Cave (1769)
Harris v Nickerson (1873)

But if the auction is stated to be 'without reserve', then this phrase is binding (*Warlow v Harrison* (1859)).

Invitation to tender

But if the invitation can be construed as a unilateral offer, it will be binding:
Harvela v Royal Trust of Canada (1985)
Blackpool & Fylde Aero Club Ltd v Blackpool BC (1990).

Termination of the offer

An offer may be terminated in one of three ways.

Revocation

- The revocation must be communicated:
  Byrne v Van Tienhoven (1880);
  but not necessarily by the offeror himself:
  Dickenson v Dodds (1876).
- An offer to keep an offer open for a certain length of time can be withdrawn like any other offer, unless an option has been purchased.
- A unilateral offer cannot be revoked when the offeree has commenced performance:
  Errington v Errington (1952)
  Daulia v Four Milbank Nominees (1978).
- Revocation of a unilateral offer to the whole world can probably be communicated by taking reasonable steps to inform the public:
  Shuey v USA (1875).

Lapse

An offer may lapse through:
- passage of time:
  Ramsgate Victoria Hotel Co v Montefiore (1866).
- death.
- failure of a condition, either express or implied:
  Financings Ltd v Stimpson (1962).

Rejection

A rejection may be either express or implied, ie:

- A counter offer
  A variation of terms or a new term will result in a counter offer:
  Hyde v Wrench (1840)
  Brogden v Metropolitan Rly Co (1877)
  Butler Machine Tool Co Ltd v Excello Corporation Ltd (1979).
  A request for further information is not a counter offer:
  Stevenson v McClean (1880).
- A conditional or qualified acceptance
  For example, the phrase 'subject to contract'.

Identification of a valid acceptance

An acceptance is a final and unqualified assent to all the terms of the offer, made by the offeree while the offer is still in force. It is a mirror image of the offer.

A person cannot accept an offer of which he or she has no knowledge:
R v Clarke (1927)
Williams v Cawardine (1833)
Tinn v Hoffman (1873).

Acceptance must be communicated

- If the offeror states a particular method of acceptance, a distinction must be drawn between mandatory and directory statements:
  Manchester Diocesan Council for Education v Commercial and General Investments Ltd (1969).
- An offeror may not stipulate that silence is to amount to acceptance:
  Felthouse v Bindley (1862).
- Prolonged silence or inactivity may in some rare cases amount to communication of acceptance:
  The Hannah Blumenthal (1983).
- Acceptance must be communicated by the offeror or his agent:
  Powell v Lee (1908).

Exceptions to the rule that acceptance must be communicated

- Where communication is expressly or impliedly waived:
  Carlill v Carbolic Smoke Ball Co (1893).

- Where failure of communication is the fault of the offeror: *Entores v Miles* (1955).
- Where the postal rule applies, ie, acceptance takes place when a letter is posted, not when it is received:
  Adams v Linsell (1818)
  Household Fire Insurance Co Ltd v Grant (1879).

The limitations to the postal rule

It must be reasonable to use the post as a means of communication: *Henthorn v Fraser* (1892).
It does not apply if the offeror has requested actual communication: *Holwell v Hughes* (1974).

Note
There are arguments as to whether an acceptance by post can be retracted.

Communication by instantaneous/electronic means

Acceptance takes place when and where the message is received:
Entores v Miles (1955)
Brinkibon v Stahag-Stahl (1983).

Certainty of terms and incomplete agreements

It is for the parties to make their own agreement. An agreement to make an agreement or an agreement that is vague will not constitute a binding contract:
Scammell & Nephew v Ouston (1941)
Walford v Miles (1992)
May & Butcher v R (1934).
But the uncertainty may be cured by
- a trade custom;
- previous dealings between the parties (*Hillas v Arcos* (1932));
- the contract itself, which provides a method for resolving an uncertainty:
  Foley v Classique Coaches (1934).
- The Sale of Goods Act 1979.

Note
The courts will ignore meaningless terms.

The court will strive to find an executed contract to be valid eg an arbitration clause validated the contract in *Foley v Classique Coaches* (an executed contract) but did not do so in *May & Butcher v R* (an unexecuted contract).

'Lock-out agreements' have been declared valid

Walford v Miles (1992)
Pitt v PHH Asset Management (1993)

2 Consideration and intention to be legally bound

You should be familiar with the following areas:	✓
• the function of consideration	
• definitions of consideration	
• kinds of consideration	
• adequacy of consideration	
• sufficiency of consideration	
• economic duress	
• promissory estoppel	
• intention to be legally bound	

The function of consideration

Most legal systems refuse to enforce promises unless there is something to indicate that the promisor intended to be bound ie some 'badge of enforceability'.

Form

Writing is a requirement in many legal systems. English law accepts form to a very limited extent as a 'badge of enforceability' in that it will enforce promises that are contained in deeds. (A deed is document which is signed and attested and indicates on its face that it is a deed.)

Reciprocity (a bargain)

Consideration is the name given to the need for reciprocity in contracts. It is the main 'badge of enforceability' in English law, 'the element of exchange in a contract'.

Reliance

An attempt has been made to introduce reliance as a basis for enforcing promises through the doctrine of promissory estoppel.

Traditionally, English law will only enforce a promise which is made under seal (a deed) or which is supported by consideration.

What is consideration?

The classic definition set down by Lush J in *Currie v Misa* (1875) is as follows:

A valuable consideration in the eyes of the law may consist either in some right, interest, profit or benefit to one party, or some forbearance, detriment, loss or responsibility given, suffered or undertaken by the other.

Shorter version:

A benefit to one party or a detriment to the other.

Limitation of the definition

The definition makes no mention of why the promisee incurs a detriment or confers a benefit, or that the element of a bargain is central to the classical notion of consideration. In *Combe v Combe* (1951) it was held that there was no consideration for the defendant's promise to pay his ex-wife £100 per year even though in reliance on that promise she had not applied to the divorce court for maintenance, and in that sense she had suffered a detriment. The reason the detriment did not constitute consideration was that there was no request by the husband, express or implied, that she should forebear from applying for maintenance.

Some writers have preferred to emphasise this element of bargain and have defined consideration as the 'element of exchange in a contract' or 'the price paid for a promise' but on the whole these are considered too vague to be really helpful.

The definition does not specify the sorts of benefit and detriment the law will regard as sufficient. It does not distinguish between factual and legal benefits. See 'Sufficiency of Consideration'.

Consideration and condition

Consideration must be distinguished from the fulfilment of a condition. If A says to B, 'I will give you £500 if you break a leg', there is no contract but simply a gratuitous promise subject to a condition. In *Carlill v Carbolic Smoke-Ball Co* (1893), the plaintiff provided consideration for the defendant's promise by using the smoke-ball. Catching influenza was only a condition of her entitlement to enforce the promise.

If A says to B, 'You can have my golf clubs if you come to collect them', there may still be only a conditional gift unless performance of the stipulation is regarded by the parties as the price paid for the promise.

Kinds of consideration

Executory

A promise to do something in the future. Mutual promises can amount to consideration for each other. A promise, however, is only regarded as consideration if its performance would also have been so regarded.

Executed

An act wholly performed at the time the contract is entered into.

Past consideration

Something already completed before the promise is made – this is not valid consideration in the eyes of the law. (The 'past consideration' rule can be seen as an example of the fact that consideration must be given in return for the promise.) In *Roscorla v Thomas* (1842), the defendant promised the plaintiff that a horse which had been bought by him was sound and free from vice. It was held that since this promise was made after the sale had been completed, there was not consideration for it and it could not be enforced. In *Re McArdle* (1951), a promise made 'in consideration of your carrying our certain improvements to the property' was held by the Court of Appeal to be unenforceable as all the work had been done before the promise was made.

Exceptions to the rule that past consideration is not good consideration

1 Where a service was rendered at the request of the promisee on the understanding that a payment would be made – a subsequent promise to pay a certain sum will be enforced on the basis that it merely identified the amount (*Lampleigh v Braithwaite* (1615)). Treitel points

out that in such cases the promisee, quite apart from the subsequent promise, is entitled to a *quantum meruit* payment for his services.

The necessary conditions for the modern version of this rule were laid down by Lord Scarman in *Pao On v Lau Yiu Long* (1980).

- The act must have taken place at the promisor's request.
- The parties must have understood that the act was to be remunerated, either by a payment, or the conferment of some other benefit.
- The payment or the conferment of benefit must have been legally enforceable.

2 Written acknowledgement of a statute barred debt will revive the debt (Limitation Act 1980).

3 Negotiable instruments (Bills of Exchange Act 1882).

Consideration must move from the promisee

Only a person who has provided consideration for a promise can enforce a promise.

In *Dunlop Pneumatic Tyre Company Ltd v Selfridge* (1915), Dunlop sold tyres to Day who resold them to Selfridge. Day, on the request of Dunlop inserted a term prohibiting Selfridge from re-selling the tyres below list price. Selfridge broke the term. Dunlop sued for breach of contract. It was held that even if Day had acted as agents for Dunlop, Dunlop could not enforce the contract as they had not provided any consideration for the promise by Selfridge. See Chapter 10 on Privity of Contract.

Consideration need not be adequate

The court will look to see whether the purported consideration contains any value (see 'Sufficiency of Consideration'). If it sees that there can be some value, then it will not concern itself with the accuracy of the valuation.

In *Mountford v Scott* (1975), £1 was paid for an option to purchase a house, and this was found to be good consideration. In *Chappell & Co v Nestle* (1960), three wrappers from the defendant's chocolate bars were found to be part of the consideration. In *Midland Bank v Green* (1981), a husband conveyed an estate to his wife at a low price to avoid the operation of an option to purchase. The court refused to look at the adequacy of the consideration.

A promise to give away onerous property is binding if the donee promises in return to discharge the obligations attached to it, eg a promise to give away a freehold house providing the donee takes over outstanding mortgage payments and other charges, *cf* conditional gifts.

Withdrawal of threatened legal proceedings will amount to consideration, even if the claim is later found to have no legal basis, provided the plaintiff believed in good faith that he was giving up something of value. In *Pitt v PHH Asset Management* (1993) the defendant agreed to a lock-out agreement in return for Pitt dropping his claim for an injunction against them. The claim for an injunction had no merit but did have a nuisance value and, therefore, did amount to consideration. The promise to exchange contracts within two weeks also had 'some value' and was, therefore, consideration as was the removal of the threat to cause trouble with another prospective buyer.

Forebearance to sue can also amount to valuable consideration. In *Alliance Bank v Broome* (1864), the defendant owed £22,000 to his bank who pressed him to provide some security. He promised to do so and as a result the bank forebore to sue. It was held that there was consideration.

It has been suggested that in some cases where the courts have discovered 'trifling consideration' in the past, the matter could now be dealt with under some other head than contract.

In *Bainbridge v Firmstone* (1838), where there had been a gratuitous bailment, the court regarded the owners parting with possession was sufficient consideration for the bailee's implied promise to return the goods in their original state. It has been suggested that this is a duty of bailment in any case, and consideration is not necessary in that case.

In *De La Bere v Pearson* (1908), the defendants owned a newspaper. They invited readers to apply by letter for free financial advice. The letters and advice were published. The advice given to the plaintiff was negligent and he lost money as a result. It was held that the plaintiff had given consideration by writing a letter which could be published. Today this claim could have been better dealt with under the heading of 'Negligent Statements in the Law of Tort'.

Note

Atiyah describes some of the above as 'invented' consideration – consideration discovered by the court although the parties themselves may not have thought of them as consideration.

There is no consideration, however, where the promises are vague eg 'to stop being a nuisance to his father' (*White v Bluett* (1853)) (but *cf* *Pitt v PHH Asset Management* above); or illusory, eg to do something impossible; or merely 'good', eg to show love or affection or gratitude.

It has been argued that, because the latter are invalid, consideration must have some economic value. But it has also been pointed out that economic value is extremely difficult to discern in the other cases cited above. Since consideration is a badge of enforceability, it is argued that nominal consideration is adequate; it is only designed to show that the promise is intended to be legally enforceable; whether it creates any economic advantage is irrelevant. Consideration, therefore, is found when a person receives whatever he requests in return for a promise whether or not it has an economic value, provided it is not too vague.

Consideration must be sufficient

Consideration must have value in the eyes of the law. Traditionally, doing something which one is legally bound to do cannot amount to consideration.

Duty imposed by the general law

Duties imposed by the general law include not taking part in a crime, or promising to appear in court after being subpœnaed. In *Collins v Godefroy* (1831), a promise to pay a fee to a witness who has been properly subpœnaed to attend a trial was held to have been made without consideration. The witness had a public duty to attend.

But if a person does, or promises to do, more than he is required to do by law, then he is providing consideration. In *Glasbrook v Glamorgan CC* (1925), the council, as police authority, sued on an agreement to pay for police protection during a strike. In the opinion of the senior police officer, a garrison was unnecessary to preserve the peace; a mobile force would have been adequate. On the insistence of the colliery manager, he agreed to provide a garrison in return for a promise of payment. It was held that the decision as to what measures were necessary to preserve the peace was the responsibility of the senior police officer on the spot, and provided it was made in good faith and reasonable, the court would not interfere with it. Thus, the police had done more than they were obliged to do and were entitled to be paid for it.

In *Ward v Byham* (1956), the father of an illegitimate child wrote to the mother from whom he was separated, saying that she could have the child and an allowance of £1 per week if she proved that the child was 'well-looked after and happy'. It was held that the mother was entitled to enforce the promise because in undertaking to see that the child was 'well-looked after and happy', she was doing more than her legal obligation. Lord Denning, however, based his decision on the ground that the mother provided consideration by performing her legal duty to maintain the child.

Treitel agrees with Denning that performance of a duty imposed by the law can be consideration for a promise. He argues that it is public policy which accounts for the refusal of the law in certain circumstances to enforce promises to perform existing duties. He claims that where there are no grounds of public policy involved, then a promise given in consideration of a public duty can be enforced.

He cites:

- promises to pay rewards for information leading to the arrest of a felon. See *Sykes v DPP* (1961) where the House of Lords held that citizens had a duty to reveal felonies known to them, and to give what information they had.
- *Ward v Byham* (above).

In most cases, it would make no difference whether the court proceeded on the basis that the matter was one of public policy or a lack of consideration. However, the former ground does allow a greater degree of flexibility.

Duty imposed by a contract with the same party

The basic rule is that if A is bound to do something by virtue of a contract with B, performance of that duty or the promise to perform that duty cannot be consideration for a further promise by B.

A request for extra payment for doing the same work

In *Stilk v Meyrick* (1809), two sailors deserted their ship; the captain promised the rest of crew extra wages if they would sail the ship back home. It was held that the crew were already bound by their contract to meet the normal emergencies of the voyage and were doing no more than their original contractual duty in working the ship home.

Where the promisor, however, performs more than he had originally promised, then there can be consideration. In *Hartley v Ponsonby* (1857), nearly half the crew deserted. This discharged the contracts of the remaining sailors as it was dangerous to sail the ship home with only half the crew. The sailors were therefore free to make a new bargain, so the captain's promise to pay them additional wages was enforceable.

Exception to the rule in *Stilk v Meyrick*

In *Williams v Roffey Bros & Nicholls* (1991), the defendants (the main contractors) were refurbishing a block of flats. They sub-contracted the carpentry work to the plaintiff. The plaintiff ran into financial difficulties, whereupon the defendants agreed to pay the plaintiff an additional sum if they completed the work on time. It was held that where a party to an existing contract later agrees to pay an 'extra bonus' in order that the other party performs his obligations under the original contract, then the new agreement is binding if the party agreeing to pay the bonus has thereby obtained some new practical advantage or avoided a disadvantage. In this particular case, the advantage was the avoidance of a penalty clause and the expense of finding new carpenters.

Stilk v Meyrick recognises as consideration only those acts which the promisor was not under a legal obligation to perform. *Williams v Roffey* adds to these, factual advantages obtained by the promisee. This decision pushes to the fore the principles of economic duress as a means of distinguishing extorted and non-extorted modifications to a contract. (See 'Economic Duress')

A request to avoid part payment of a debt

The basic rule is such that payment of a smaller sum will not discharge the duty to pay a higher sum (*Pinnel's Case* (1602)). If a creditor is owed £100 and agrees to accept £90 in full settlement, he can later insist on the remaining £10 being paid since there is no consideration for his promise to waive the £10.

The rule in *Pinnel's* case was confirmed by the House of Lords in *Foakes v Beer* (1884). Dr Foakes was indebted to Mrs Beer on a judgment sum of £2,090. It was agreed by Mrs Beer that if Foakes paid her £500 in cash and the balance of £1,590 in instalments, she would not take 'any proceedings whatsoever' on the judgment. Foakes paid the money exactly as requested, but Mrs Beer then proceeded to claim an additional £360 as interest on the judgment debt. Foakes refused and when sued, pleaded that his duty to pay interest had been discharged by the promise not to sue. Their Lordships deferred as to whether, on its true construction, the agreement merely gave Foakes time to pay or was intended to cover interest as well. But they held, even on the latter construction, there was no consideration for the promise and that Foakes was still bound to pay the additional sum.

There are situations, however, where payment of a smaller sum will discharge the liability for the higher sum, for example:

- where the promise to accept a smaller sum in full settlement is made by deed, or in return for consideration;
- where the original claim was unliquidated or disputed in good faith;
- where the debtor does something different, ie where payment is made, at the creditor's request
(a)   at an earlier time,
(b)   at a different place,
(c)   by a different method (it was held in *DC Builders Ltd v Rees* (1966) that payment by cheque is not payment by a different method),
(d)   where payment is accompanied by a benefit of some kind.

Consideration can be identified in the above cases. It is more difficult, however, in the next two situations which are probably genuine exceptions to the rule:

(e)   in a composition agreement with creditors,
(f)   where payment is made by a third party (see *Hirachand Punachand v Temple* (1911)).

It has been argued that to allow the creditor to sue for the remaining debt would be a fraud on the third parties in the above two cases.

The doctrine of promissory estoppel, under certain circumstances, may allow payment of a smaller sum to discharge liability for the larger sum.

Duties owed to third party

Where a duty is owed to a third party, its performance can also be consideration for a promise by another. It is clear that the third party is getting something more than he is entitled to.

In *Shadwell v Shadwell* (1860), an uncle promised to pay an annual sum to his nephew on hearing of his intended marriage. Although the court found consideration for the uncle's promise it is generally considered unconvincing. Admittedly, the nephew was already engaged to Ellen Nicholl, but the uncle had no right to demand that the nephew should marry Ellen and his doing so at his uncle's request would have provided consideration.

In *Scotson v Pegg* (1861), A agreed to deliver coal to B's order. B ordered A to deliver coal to C who promised A to unload it. It was held that A could enforce C's promise since A's delivery of the coal was good consideration, notwithstanding that A was already bound to do so by the contract with B.

In *New Zealand Shipping Co Ltd v AM Satterthwaite & Co Ltd The Eurymedon* (1975), it was held by the Privy Council that where a stevedore, at the request of the shipper of the goods, removed the goods from a ship, this was consideration for the promise by the shipper not to sue him for damages, although the stevedore in removing the goods was only performing contractual duties he owed to the shipper.

Note

The rule that doing what you are legally bound to do cannot be consideration is under challenge in all its aspects.

Performing a statutory duty has been asserted by Treitel and Lord Denning as sufficient consideration (see above).

Stilk v Meyrick now has an exception in *Williams v Roffey Bros* which indicates that performing an existing contractual duty can amount to consideration for a promise of extra payment providing the promisor receives an actual, as distinct from a legal, advantage.

Part payment of a debt cannot amount to consideration, nor an actual advantage as in *Williams v Roffey* (*Re Selectmore* (1994)), but promissory estoppel may prevent the promisor from going back on his promise.

Performing an existing contractual duty will, in any case, be consideration if the first contractual duty was to a third party.

It is sometimes asserted that the doctrine of consideration ignores economic reality, on the basis that:

- it is very difficult to identify any economic benefit in the cases listed under the adequacy of consideration (see above);
- the rules in *Stilk v Meyrick* and *Foakes v Beer* insist on legal benefits and ignore the economic benefits which might be present. Now, however, *Williams v Roffey* does recognise an actual economic benefit as consideration.

Promissory estoppel

The basis of the doctrine

In *Central London Property Trust Ltd v High Trees House Ltd* (1947) the plaintiffs let a block of flats to the defendants. In January 1940, they agreed to accept half-rent since many of the flats were unlet. In 1945 the flats were all let and the plaintiffs claimed full rent again. Lord Denning held that the arrangement was only intended to last during the war and gave judgment for the plaintiffs. He also stated that if the plaintiffs had sought to recover past rents, they would have failed. They would, he said, be estopped by their promise from asserting their legal right to demand payment.

He based his judgment on *Hughes v Metropolitan Rly Co* (1877) where Lord Cairns stated:

Where one party leads the other to suppose that the strict rights arising under the contract will not be enforced ... the person who otherwise might have enforced those rights will not be allowed to enforce them where it would be inequitable.

This doctrine of promissory estoppel, promulgated by Lord Denning, has been the subject of much controversy. It is argued that it is contrary to two House of Lords' decisions. In *Jordan v Money* (1854) the House of Lords had stated that only a representation of fact was ground for estoppel. It is argued by Lord Denning that *Hughes v Metropolitan Rly* created an exception to *Jorden v Money*, where the parties were already in a contractual relationship; and that in any case the promise in *Jorden v Money* was not intended to be legally binding. The dicta of Lord Denning is also contrary to the decision of the House of Lords in *Foakes v Beer*. It is argued by Lord Denning that estoppel was not pleaded in *Foakes v Beer*, and that the entitlement to the money had already accrued in *Foakes v Beer*.

The scope of the doctrine

- The doctrine must relate to a modification of an existing right – see *Combe v Combe* (above) where Lord Denning stated, 'The principle does not create a new course of action – it only prevents a party from insisting on his strict legal rights.'
  Following *Crabb v Arun DC* (1976) where proprietory estoppel was allowed to create new rights, Lord Denning favoured the merging of the two forms of equitable estoppel, thus allowing promissory estoppel to create new rights. However, other judges and academic authorities have insisted that they are separate and that promissory estoppel does not create new rights.
  (Cf the Australian case of *Waltons v Maher* (1988) where promissory estoppel was allowed to create new rights on the basis that it would be unconscionable to allow the promisor to go back on his promise.)
- The promise must be 'clear and unequivocal'. In *The Scaptrade* (1983) a vessel was chartered and payment was to be made on the 8th day of the month. If payment was not made on time the owners could withdraw. On some months payment was late, but the owners did not withdraw. However, on a subsequent late payment the

owners did withdraw. The hirers pleaded equitable estoppel. It was held that there was no clear and unequivocal promise by the owners and in any event it was not inequitable for the owners to withdraw, since the owners conduct had not caused the charterers to make late payments.

- It must be inequitable to allow the promisor to go back on his promise and revert to his legal rights. In *D&C Builders v Rees* (1966) the debtors took advantage of the creditors' financial problems to pressure them into accepting part-payment. Lord Denning held that in this case, it would not be inequitable for the creditors to go back on their promise to accept the payment in full settlement. (See also *The Scaptrade* (above).)

- The promisee must have acted in reliance on the promise. There is some uncertainty as to whether the promisee must have acted to his detriment. Several High Court judges have referred to 'detriment'. Lord Denning, however, stated in *Alan & Co Ltd v El-Nasr Export and Import Co* (1972) that detriment was not necessary, 'He must have acted differently, that is the test.' There was no detriment in the *High Trees House* case, but there was detriment in *Hughes v Metropolitan Railway*.

Is the doctrine suspensory or extinctive in its effect?

It has never been conclusively determined whether the doctrine may be applied to extinguish permanently the right to the balance of a debt, or whether it merely suspends the creditors' rights until such time as it is equitable to claim the balance.

In *The High Trees House* case the instalments of rent due during the war were considered extinguished, but the right to claim the full rent for future periods was only suspended. In *Tool Metal Manufacturing Co Ltd v Tungsten Electric Co Ltd* (1955) the owner of a patent promised to suspend periodic payments during the war. It was held by the Court of Appeal that the promise was binding for the duration of the war but the owners could, on giving reasonable notice at the end of the war, revert to their original legal entitlements. In *Ajayi v Briscoe* (1964) the Privy Council stated that the promisee could resile from his promise on giving reasonable notice which allowed the promisee a reasonable opportunity of resuming his position, but that the promise would become final if the promisee could not resume his former position.

On one interpretation, these cases reveal that with regard to existing, or past obligations, it is extinctive; but with regard to future obligations it is suspensory.

On another interpretation, the correct approach is to look at the nature of the promise. If it was intended to be permanent, then the promisees' liability will be extinguished. Lord Denning has consistently asserted that promissory estoppel can extinguish debts. However, this view is contrary to *Foakes v Beer*. The view that promissory estoppel is suspensory only would reconcile it with the decisions in *Jorden v Money*, *Foakes v Beer* and *Pinnel's* case, but it would deprive it of most of its usefulness.

The question of whether the doctrine is suspensory or extinctive is particularly important with regard to single payments.

Status of the doctrine

Promissory estoppel has been widely discussed, but rarely applied.

It was not applied in *The High Trees House Case* (1947) and *Combe v Combe* and *D & C Builders v Rees*.

It was applied by Lord Denning, but other judges reached the same conclusion on other grounds in *Alan v El Nasr* and *Brikom Investments Ltd v Carr* (1979).

Promissory estoppel was applied by the Court of Appeal in *Tool Metal Manufacturing Co Ltd v Tungsten Electric Co Ltd*.

Lord Hailsham, when Lord Chancellor, called for the cases to be reviewed and reduced to a coherent body of doctrine by the House of Lords.

Intention to be legally bound

Traditionally, English law has required the parties to a contract to have intended to create legal relations.

In commercial and business agreements there is a presumption that the parties intend to create legal relations

This presumption may be rebutted but the onus of proof is on the party seeking to exclude legal relations. In *Esso Petroleum Ltd v Commissioners of Custom and Excise* (1976), Esso promised to give one world cup coin with every four gallons of petrol sold. A majority in the House of Lords believed that the presumption in favour of legal relations had not been rebutted.

Examples of rebuttal

- 'Agreement may not be subject to the jurisdiction of any court' (*Rose & Frank v Crompton Bros* (1925))
- Agreements to be binding 'in honour only' (*Jones v Vernon Pools* (1938)).
- Letters of comfort ie statements to encourage lending to an associated company.

It was held in *Kleinwort Benson Ltd v Malaysia Mining Corp* (1989) that the defendant's statement that 'it is our policy to ensure that the business is at all times in a position to meet its liabilities to you', was a statement of present fact and not a promise for the future. It was not intended to create legal relations.

Collective agreements are declared not to be legally binding by TULRA 1974.

In social and domestic agreements there is a presumption against legal relations

This can be rebutted by evidence to the contrary, for example:

- Agreements between husband and wife
  In *Balfour v Balfour* (1919) the court refused to enforce a promise by the husband to give his wife £50 per month whilst he was working abroad. However, the court will enforce a clear agreement where the parties are separating or separated (*Merritt v Merritt* (1970)).
- Agreements between members of a family
  In *Jones v Padavatton* (1969) Mrs Jones offered a monthly allowance to her daughter if she would come to England to read for the Bar. Her daughter agreed but was not very successful. Mrs Jones stopped paying the monthly allowance but allowed her daughter to live in her house and receive the rents from other tenants. Mrs Jones later sued for possession. The daughter counter-claimed for breach of the agreement to pay the monthly allowance and/or for accommodation. It was held that (a) the first agreement may have been made with the intention of creating legal relations, but was for a reasonable time and would, in any case, have lapsed, and (b) the second agreement was a family arrangement without an intention to create legal relations. It was very vague and uncertain.

But intention may be inferred where one party has acted to his detriment on the agreement (*Parker v Clarke* (1960)) or where a business arrangement is involved (*Snelling v Snelling* (1973)) or where there is mutuality (*Simkins v Pays* (1955)).

But in all such cases, the agreement must be clear.

Revision Notes

Consideration is the normal 'badge of enforceability' in English law.

Definitions of consideration

'A benefit to one party or a detriment to another'
'The price paid for a promise'
'The element of exchange in a contract'

For the difference between consideration and condition see *Carlill v Carbolic Smoke Ball Co Ltd* (1983).

Kinds of consideration

- Executory – a promise to do something in the future.
- Executed – an act wholly performed at the time the contract is entered into.

Past consideration – something already completed before the promise is made cannot amount to consideration:
Roscorla v Thomas (1842)
Re McArdle (1971).

Exceptions

Where a service is rendered at the request of the promisee, on the understanding that a payment will be made, a subsequent promise to pay a certain sum will be enforced provided that the payment would be legally enforceable if it had been promised in advance (*Pao On v Lau Yiu Long* (1980)).

Rules governing consideration

Consideration must move from the promisee

Only a person who has provided consideration for a promise can enforce that promise (*Dunlop v Selfridge* (1915)).

Consideration need not be adequate

Adequacy is a question of fact. It need not equal in value the consideration provided by the other party. It is for the parties themselves to make their own bargain:
Chappel Co Ltd v Nestle Co Ltd (1960)
Pitt v PHH Asset Management (1993).
'Trifling' consideration was held valid in *De La Bere v Pearson* (1908).

Consideration must be sufficient

Sufficiency is a question of law. The consideration must have some value in the eyes of the law.
Traditionally, the following have no value in the eyes of the law:
• A promise to perform an existing public duty
  Collins v Godefroy (1831).
  If he does more than his duty, then there is consideration
  Glasbrook Bros v Glamorgan CC (1926)
  Ward v Byham (1956).
• A promise to fulfil an existing duty owed to the same person eg
  (a)   A request for extra payment
        It was held in *Stilk v Meyrick* (1809) that performing an existing contractual duty was not consideration for a promise of extra money. This was confirmed in the *Atlantic Baron* (1978). But if more than had originally been promised is performed, then there is consideration (*Hartley v Ponsonby* (1857)).

        Exception to the rule in Stilk v Meyrick
        In *Williams v Roffey Bros & Nicholls* (1989) the Court of Appeal recognised as consideration, factual advantages obtained by the promisor in addition to the legal advantages required in *Stilk v Meyrick*.
        'Economic duress' now becomes important as a means of preventing extorted modifications to a contract.
  (b)   A request to avoid part-payment of a debt.
        The basic rule is that payment of a smaller sum will not discharge the duty to pay the higher sum:
        Pinnel's Case (1602)
        Foakes v Beer (1884).
        There will be consideration, however, where:
        • The original sum was unliquidated or disputed in good faith; or
        • The payment was made at the creditors request

(a)   at an earlier time;
(b)   at a different place;
(c)   by a different method (it was held in *D&C Builders v Rees* (1966) that payment by cheque was not payment by a different method);
(d)   by a third party (*Hirachand Punachand v Temple* (1911));
(e)   as part of a composition agreement between creditors.

Note
The doctrine of promissory estoppel under certain circumstances estopps a promisor from going back on his promise to accept a smaller sum in discharge of a larger sum (see below).

Performance of a contractual duty already owed to a third party can amount to valuable consideration:
Scotson v Pegg (1961)
Shadwell v Shadwell (1861)
The Eurymedon (1974).

Promissory estoppel

If a promise intended to be be binding is acted upon, then the court will not allow the promisor to go back on his promise.

There are problems with regard to the origins of the doctrine and its scope.

Origins

It was introduced by Lord Denning in the *Central London Property Trust Ltd v High Trees House Ltd* (1947) and was based on the decision in *Hughes v Metropolitan Rly* (1877)

It would seem to conflict with the House of Lords' decisions in *Jordan v Money* (1854) and *Foakes v Beer* (1884).

Scope

The exact scope of the doctrine is a matter of debate, but certain requirements must be met.
• It only applies to the modification or discharge of an existing contractual obligation. It cannot create a new contract:
    Combe v Combe (1951)
    Brikom Investments v Carr (1979).

- It can be used as a 'shield and not a sword'
  But see Australian case of *Waltons v Maher* (1988)
- The promise must be clear and unequivocal:
  The Scaptrade (1983).
- It must be inequitable for the promisor to go back on his promise:
  D&C Builders v Rees (1966).
- The promisee must have acted in reliance on the promise, although not necessarily to his detriment:
  Alan & Co Ltd v El-Nasr Export & Import Co Ltd (1972).

Effect of the doctrine

It is not clear whether the doctrine extinguishes rights or merely suspends them.

In *Tool Metal Tungsten v Tungsten Electric Co Ltd* (1955) it extinguished past rights, but allowed future rights to be re-instated on the giving of reasonable notice.

If it is suspensory only, then it can be reconciled with *Foakes v Beer* but much of its usefulness will be lost.

Intention to be legally bound

Commercial agreements are presumed to be legally binding, but the presumption may be rebutted by evidence to the contrary:
Rose & Frank v Crompton Bros (1925)
Jones v Vernon Pools (1939)
Kleinwort Benson Ltd v Malaysian Mining Corp (1989).

Social and domestic agreements are presumed not to be legally binding but the presumption may be rebutted by evidence to the contrary:
Balfour v Balfour (1919)
Merritt v Merritt (1970)
Jones v Padavatton (1969)
Parker v Clarke (1960)
Snelling v Snelling (1973)
Simkins v Pays (1955).

In both cases the burden of proof is on the person seeking to rebut the presumption.

3 Contents of a contract

ESSENTIALS

You should be familiar with the following areas:	✓
• distinction between terms and mere representations	
• interpretation of the express terms of a contract	
• identification of the implied terms	
• the different weighting given to different terms	

Once the existence of a contract has been confirmed, it is necessary to explore the scope of the obligations which each party incur. Three aspects call for special attention.

The distinction between terms and mere representations

Is the statement or assurance a part of the contract? Statements made during negotiations leading to a contract may be either:

Terms

These are statements which form the express terms of the contract. If these are untrue, the untruth constitutes a breach of contract.

Mere representations

These are statements which do not form part of the contract, but which help to induce the contract. If these are untrue, they are 'misrepresentations'.

Now that damages can be awarded for negligent misrepresentation, the distinction has lost much of its former importance. However, it does retain some significance as the right to damages for breach of contract differs in a number of ways from the right to damages for misrepresentation.

Whether a statement has become a term of the contract, depends on the intention of the parties. In trying to ascertain such intention, the court may take into account the following factors:

- The importance of the statement to the parties
  In *Bannerman v White* (1861) the buyer stated 'if sulphur has been used, I do not want to know the price'. It was held to be a term. Similarly, in *Couchman v Hill* (1947) the buyer asked if the cow was in calf, stating that if she was, he would not bid. The auctioneer's reply that she was not in calf was held to be a term, overriding the printed conditions which stated that no warranty was given (*Routledge v McKay* (1954)).
- The respective knowledge of the parties
  In *Oscar Chess Ltd v Williams* (1957) it was held that a statement by a member of the public (a non-expert) to a garage (an expert) with regard to the age of a car was a mere representation not a term. On the other hand a statement made by a garage (an expert) to a member of the public (a non-expert) concerning the mileage of a car was held to be a term (*Dick Bentley Productions Ltd v Harold Smith (Motors) Ltd* (1965)).
- The manner of the statement
  For example, if it suggests verification (*Ecay v Godfrey* (1947)) it is unlikely to be a term. If it discourages verification 'If there was anything wrong with the horse, I would tell you' (*Schawel v Reade* (1913)) it is likely to be a term.
- Where a contract has been reduced to writing
  The terms will normally be the statements incorporated into the written contract (*Routledge v McKay* (1954)).
  A contract may, however, be partly oral and partly written (*Couchman v Hill* (1947)). In *Evans & Sons Ltd v Andrea Merzario Ltd* (1976) an oral assurance that machinery would be stowed under, not on, the deck was held to be a term of a contract, although it was not incorporated into the written terms. The court held that the contract was partly oral, and partly written and in such hybrid circumstances the court was entitled to look at all the circumstances.

Note
The discovery of a collateral contract may overcome the difficulties of oral warranties in written contracts. In *City & Westminster Properties v Mudd* (1959) a tenant signed a lease containing a covenant to use the premises for business premises only. He was induced to sign by a statement that this clause did not apply to him and that he could continue to sleep on the premises. The court found that his signing the

contract was consideration for this promise, thus creating a collateral contract. In *Evans & Son Ltd v Andrea Merzario Ltd* (1976) Lord Denning considered the oral statement to be a collateral contract. In *Esso Petroleum v Mardon* (1976) the court held that the statement by a representative of Esso with regard to the throughput of a petrol station was covered by an implied collateral warranty that the statement had been made with due care and skill. Acceptance by the court of a collateral contract is, however, rare. It was stated by Lord Moulton in *Heilbut, Symons Ltd v Buckleton* (1913): 'Not only the terms of such contracts, but the existence of an *animus contrahendi* on the part of all parties to them must be strictly shown'.

Identification of express terms of a contract

See Incorporation of terms (Chapter 4).

Interpretation of express terms of a contract

Oral contracts

The contents are a matter of evidence for the judge. The interpretation will be undertaken by applying the objective rule (*Thake v Maurice* (1986)).

Written contracts

If a contract is reduced to writing then under the 'Parol Evidence' rule, oral or other evidence extrinsic to the document is not normally admissible to 'add to, vary, or contradict', the terms of the written agreement.

Exceptions
- To show that the contract is not legally binding, eg because of mistake or misrepresentation.
- To show that the contract is subject to a 'condition precedent'. In *Pym v Cambell* (1856) oral evidence was admitted to show that a contract was not to come into operation unless a patent was approved by a third party.

- To establish a custom or trade usage (*Hutton v Warren* (1836) see below).
- To establish that the written contract is not the whole contract. It is presumed that 'a document which looks like a contract is the whole contract', but this is rebuttable (see *Couchman v Hill* (1947) and *Evans v Andrea Merzario*).
  A contract may be contained in more than one document (*Jacobs v Batavia Plantation Trust Ltd* (1924)).
- To establish a collateral contract (*City & Westminster Properties Ltd v Mudd* (1959); *Evans & Son Ltd v Andrea Merzario Ltd* (1976)).

The Law Commission recommended in 1976 that the 'Parol Evidence' rule be abolished. However, in view of the wide exceptions to the rule, it recommended in 1986 that no action need be taken.

Identification of implied terms

In addition to the terms which the parties have expressly agreed, a court may be prepared to hold that other terms must be implied into the contract. Such terms may be implied from one of three sources.

Custom

A contract may be deemed to incorporate any relevant custom of the market, trade or locality in which the contract is made. In *Hutton v Warren* (1836) a tenant established a right to fair allowance for improvements to the land through a local custom.

Statute

Parliament, as a matter of public policy, has in numerous instances, seen fit to imply terms into contracts, for example:
- The Sale of Goods Act 1979 which implies the following terms into all contracts for the sale of goods:
- (a) That the seller has the right to sell the goods.
- (b) That goods sold by description correspond with the description.
  In a sale by way of business:
- (a) That the goods are of merchantable quality.
- (b) That the goods are fit for any special purpose made known to the seller.
- (c) That goods sold by sample correspond with the sample.

- The Supply of Goods and Services Act 1982 implies similar terms into contracts of hire, contracts for work and materials, and other contracts not covered by the Sale of Goods Act.
  In contracts of service, there is an implied term that the service will be carried out with reasonable care and skill, within a reasonable time, and for a reasonable price.
- The Consumer Credit Act 1974.
- The Marine Insurance Act 1906.

The courts

Terms implied in fact
The court seeks to give effect to the unexpressed intention of the parties. There are two tests. A term may be implied because:
- It is necessary to give business efficacy to the contract
  In *The Moorcock* (1889) a term was implied that the riverbed was in a condition that would not damage a ship unloading at the jetty.
- It satisfies the 'officious bystander' test, ie if a bystander suggested a term, the parties would respond with a common 'of course'. In *Spring v NASDS* (1956) the union tried to imply the 'Bridlington Agreement'. The court refused on the basis that if an officious bystander had suggested this, the plaintiff would have replied 'What's that?'

The *Moorcock* doctrine is used in order to make the contract workable, or where it was so obvious that the parties must have intended it to apply to the agreement. It will not be used merely because it was reasonable or because it would improve the contract.

Terms implied in law
The court implies certain terms into all contracts of a particular kind. Here the court is not trying to put into effect the parties intention, but is imposing an obligation on one party, often as a matter of public policy eg the court implies into all contracts of employment a term that the employee will carry out his work with reasonable care and skill and will indemnify his employer against any loss caused by his negligence (*Lister v Romford Ice Cold Storage Co Ltd* (1957)). In these cases, the implication is not based on the presumed intention of the parties, but on the court's perception of the nature of the relationship between the parties, and whether such an implied term was reasonable.

In *Liverpool City Council v Irwin* (1977) the tenants of a block of council flats failed to persuade the court to imply a term that the council should be responsible for the common parts of the building on the *Moorcock* or 'officious bystander' test, but succeeded on the basis of the 'Lister' test ie the term should be implied in law in that the agreement was incomplete. It involved the relationship of landlord and tenant and it would be reasonable to expect the landlord to be responsible for the common parts of the building.

Classification of terms

There is a very important distinction between those terms of a contract which entitle an innocent party to terminate (rescind or treat as discharged) a contract in the event of a breach, and those which merely enable a person to claim damages.

Traditionally, a distinction has been made in English law between conditions and warranties.

Conditions

Conditions are statements of fact or promises which form the essential terms of the contract. A condition is a term which goes to the root of the contract. If the statement is not true, or the promise is not fulfilled, the injured party may terminate (or treat as discharged) the contract and claim damages, for example:

- The Sale of Goods Act 1979 designates certain implied terms, eg re merchantable quality, as conditions – the breach of which entitles the buyer to terminate (or treat as discharged) the contract.
- In *Poussard v Spiers & Pond* (1876) a singer was employed to take the lead in an opera. She was unable to take up the role until a week after the season had started. In the meantime the management had engaged another singer to take over the role for the whole season. It was held that her promise to perform from the first performance was a condition and its breach entitled the management to treat the contract as discharged.

Warranties

Warranties are contractual terms concerning the less important or subsidiary statements of facts or promises. If a warranty is broken, this does not entitle the other party to terminate (or treat as discharged) the contract, it merely entitles him to sue for damages, for example:

- The Sale of Goods Act 1979 designates certain terms as warranties, the breach of which does not allow the buyer to treat the contract as discharged, but merely to sue for damages, eg the right to quiet enjoyment.
- In *Bettini v Gye* (1876) a singer was engaged to sing for a whole season. He undertook to arrive six days in advance to take part in rehearsals. He only arrived three days in advance. In the meantime the management had engaged another singer to replace him for the whole season. It was held that the rehearsal clause was subsidiary to the main clause. It was only a warranty. The management was therefore not entitled to treat the contract as discharged and employ a replacement singer. They should have kept to the original contract and merely sought damages for the three days delay.

Innominate or intermediate terms

In *Hong Kong Fir Shipping v Kaw Aski Kisen Kaisha* (1962), however, it was suggested by the Court of Appeal that it was not enough to classify terms into conditions and warranties. Regard should also be had to the character and nature of the breach itself. Innominate or intermediate terms were discussed. The defendants chartered the vessel *Hong Kong Fir* for the plaintiffs for 24 months; the charter-party provided that 'she was fitted in every way for ordinary cargo service'. It transpired that the engine room staff were incompetent, and that the vessel spent less than nine weeks of the first seven months at sea because of breakdowns and the consequent repairs which were necessary.

Held

The term was neither a condition nor a warranty, and in determining whether the defendants could terminate the contract, it was necessary to look at the consequences of the breach to see if it deprived the innocent party of substantially the whole benefit they should have received under the contract. On the facts, this was not the case because the charter-party still had a substantial time to run. Diplock LJ stated:

There are, however, many contractual undertakings of a more complex character which cannot be categorised as being 'conditions' or 'warranties' ... of such undertakings all that can be said is that some breaches will and other will not give rise to an event which will 'deprive the party not in default of substantially the whole benefit which it was intended he should obtain from the contract' and the legal consequences of a breach of such an undertaking, unless provided for expressly in the contract, depend on the nature of the event to which the breach gives rise and do not follow automatically from a prior classification of the undertaking as a condition or warranty.

After the *Hong Kong Fir* case (1962), there was some confusion as to whether the breach based test which applied to innominate terms had replaced the term based test which relied on the distinction between conditions and warranties, or merely added an alternative to it in certain circumstances.

In the *Mihalis Angelos* (1971) the Court of Appeal reverted to the term based test. The owners of a vessel stated that the vessel was 'expected ready to load' on or about 1 July. It was discovered that this was not so. It was held that the term was a condition and the charterers could treat the contract as discharged.

The court relied on the previous case of *Benn v Burgess* (1843) where a similar 'readiness to load' term had been held a condition.

In 1976, two cases were decided on the breach based principle.

In *Cehave NV v Bremer Handelgesellschaft MBH* (1976) (*The Hansa Nord*) the seller had sold a cargo of citrus pellets with a term in the contract that the shipment be made in good condition. The buyer rejected the cargo on the basis that this term had been broken. The defect, however, was not serious, and the court held that although the Sale of Goods Act had classified some terms as conditions and warranties, it did not follow that all the terms had to be so classified. Accordingly, the court could consider the effect of the breach, and since this was not serious, the buyer had not been entitled to reject.

In *Reardon Smith v Hansen Tangen* (1976) an oil tanker was described as 'Osaka No 354', when in fact it was 'Oshine No 004', but was otherwise exactly as specified. Because the market for oil tankers had collapsed the charterers sought to argue that the number was a condition which would enable them to repudiate the contract. The House of Lords rejected this argument and held that the statement was an innominate term, not a condition – since the effect of the breach was trivial and did not justify termination of the contract.

The relationship between the two tests, the term based test and the breach based test, was explained by the House of Lords in *Bunge v Tradax* (1981) where, on the fact of the case, the House of Lords held that stipulations with regard to time will generally be held to be conditions in a mercantile contract and the innocent party could treat the contract as discharged if the condition was not complied with. Their Lordships stated that if a term is a condition, then breach of that term will allow the other party to treat the contract as discharged. The time for determining whether a clause was a condition or an innominate term was at the time of contracting, not after the breach.

Traditionally, a term is a condition if it has been established as such:
- By statute
  The Sale of Goods Act 1979.
- By precedent after a judicial decision
  In the *Mihalis Angelos* (1971) the Court of Appeal held that the 'expected readiness' clause in a charter party is a condition.
- By the intention of the parties
  The court must ascertain the intention of the parties. If the wording clearly reveals that the parties intended that breach of a particular term should give rise to a right to rescind, that term will be regarded as a condition. In *Lombard North Central plc v Butterworth* (1987) the Court of Appeal held that contracting parties can provide expressly in the contract that specific breaches which would not of themselves go to the root of the contract but may, nevertheless, be treated as if they do. In that case, the contract included an express clause that the time for payment of instalments was of the essence of the contract. An accountant had agreed to hire a computer for five years, agreeing to make an initial payment and 19 quarterly rental payments. He was late in paying some instalments, and the owners terminated the agreement, recovered possession of the computer, and claimed damages not only for the arrears, but also for loss of future instalments. The claim succeeded because the contract specifically stated that the time of payment of each instalment was to be of the essence of the contract.
  However, the mere use of the word 'condition' is not conclusive.
  In *Schuler v Wickman Machine Tool Sales Ltd* (1974) the House of Lords held that breach of a 'condition' that a distributor should visit six customers a week could not have been intended to allow rescission. The word 'condition' had not been used in this particular sense. There was in the contract a separate clause which indicated when and how the contract could be terminated.

- By the court
  Deciding according to the subject matter of the contract. See *Poussard v Spiers & Pond* (1876) and *Bettini v Gye* (1876).

If a term is not a condition, then the 'wait and see' technique can be used to decide if the gravity of the breach is such that it deprives the innocent party of substantially the whole benefit of the contract. If so, then the innocent party can terminate the contract (innominate or intermediate term).

Replacement of two fold classification by three fold classification

It is generally accepted that the two fold classification of terms into conditions and warranties was replaced in the *Hong Kong Fir* case by a three fold classification into conditions, warranties, and innominate terms. However, it has been suggested that, although not discussed, this three fold classification had been applied in practice in earlier decisions.

- In *Bunge v Tradax*, Lord Scarman spoke of innominate terms being 'rediscovered' in *Hong Kong Fir*.
- It is argued that in *Poussard v Spiers & Pond* (1876) and *Bettini v Gye* (1876) which are cited as examples of the distinction between conditions and warranties, the courts looked in fact at the effect of the breaches (breach based test) rather than at the nature of the term broken.
- It is suggested that only the name is really new.
- It has also been suggested by some writers that there are now not three types of terms but two, ie conditions, whose breach gives rise to the right to terminate other terms, whose breach allows the other party at least to sue for damages, but may also, if sufficiently fundamental, allow him to terminate.

There is no need under this view for a distinction between warranties and innominate terms because even for warranties the option to terminate should be available for particularly bad or flagrant breaches.

This view seems to have been supported by Lord Justice Omrod in *The Hansa Nord*.

It is also argued, however, that this view, although attractive, does not reflect the current position, for instance:

- *Hong Kong Fir* clearly envisaged at three fold classification.
- The Sale of Goods Act designates certain terms as warranties - leading only to damages.

It is also argued that, as a matter of policy, amalgamating innominate terms and warranties would be to deprive contracting parties of a distinction they might wish to utilise.

Certainty and flexibility

Certainty

The term based test is alleged to have the advantage of predictability and certainty. For the parties to know their legal rights and liabilities, the nature of the term is crucial, particularly as regards the availability of termination. The character of all terms is ascertainable at the moment the contract is concluded. Nothing that happens after its formation can change the status of a term. If the term is a condition then the parties will know that its breach allows the other party to terminate, eg where the term is designated a condition by legislation or by precedent or by the parties themselves. But there can still be uncertainty where the parties have to await the court's decision on the nature of the term.

Flexibility

The breach based test is stated to bring flexibility to the law. Instead of saying that the innocent party can, in the case of a condition, always terminate, or in the case of a warranty, never terminate, innominate terms allow the courts to permit termination where the circumstances justify it and the consequences are sufficiently serious.

Note

The distinction between the different types of contract terms remains of considerable importance.

Revision Notes

Terms and representations

Whether a statement is a term or a representation depends on the intention of the parties.

Guidelines for ascertaining the intention of the parties:

- The strength of the statement:
  Bannerman v White (1861)
  Couchman v Hill (1947).
- The respective knowledge of the parties:
  Oscar Chess v Williams (1957)
  Dick Bentley Productions v Harold Smith Motors Ltd (1965).
- The manner of the statement:
  Ecay v Godfrey (1947)
  Schawel v Read (1913).
- Whether the statement was reduced to writing:
  Evans & Sons Ltd v Andrea Merzario Ltd (1976).

Note
The discovery of a collateral contract may solve the problem of representations in written contracts (*City & Westminster Properties Ltd v Mudd* (1959)).
A collateral contract, however, must be strictly proven.

The interpretation of any term expressly agreed

Oral contracts – a question of evidence.
Written contracts – the 'parol evidence' rule states that oral or other evidence is not admissible to 'add to, vary or contradict' the terms of written agreement. However, evidence is allowed to establish:

- a mistake or misrepresentation.
- a condition precedent:
  Pym v Cambell (1856).
- a custom or trade usage:
  Hutton v Warren (1836).
- the written contract is not the whole contract:
  Evans v Andrea Merzario Ltd (1876).

- a collateral contract:
  City & Westminster Properties v Mudd (1959).

Incorporation of express terms in a contract
See 'Incorporation of Terms' (Chapter 4).

Implied terms

Terms may be implied into a contract by custom, statute, or the courts.

By custom
Hutton v Warren (1836)

By statute
The Sale of Goods Act 1979
The Sale and Supply of Goods Act 1982

By the court

- On the *Moorcock* principle (implied in fact)
  The court gives effect to the unexpressed intention of the parties.

  Tests
  (a)　The 'business efficacy' test. It must be necessary in order to give business efficacy to the contract.
  (b)　The 'officious bystander' test. If a bystander were to ask whether a term was included, both parties would respond with a common 'of course'.

  Terms may not be implied on the *Moorcock* principle on the basis of reasonableness.
- On the *Lister* principle (implied in law)
  The court implies certain terms into all contracts of a particular kind eg employment contracts, regardless of whether the parties intended such terms.

  Tests
  (a)　The nature of the relationship between the parties.
  (b)　Terms may be implied originally on the basis of reasonability: *Liverpool City Council v Irwin* (1977).

Classification of terms

How and why the major or essential undertakings are distinguished from minor or inessential ones.

Some breaches allow the other party to terminate the contract and sue for damages. Other breaches only allow the other party to sue for damages.

Conditions

These are terms that go to the root of the contract (Sale of Goods Act 1979; *Poussard v Spiers & Pond* (1876)).

Breach of a condition allows the other party to terminate the contract.

Warranties

These are minor or subsidiary terms (Sale of Goods Act 1979; *Bettini v Guy* (1876)).

A breach of warranty does not allow the other party to terminate the contract.

Innominate terms

These are neither conditions nor warranties (*Hong Kong Fir Case* (1961)).

Breach of innominate term may allow the other party to terminate the contract, provided it deprives the other party of substantially the whole benefit he should have had under contract.

Effect of a breach

First, it must be ascertained whether the term broken is a condition. If so, then the other party may terminate the contract.

If it is not a condition then it is probably an innominate term and the effect of the breach must be considered in order to decide whether the contract may be terminated.

Identification of terms

A condition may be identified:
- By statute:
  The Sale of Goods Act 1979.

- By precedent:
  Bunge v Tradax (1981).
- By the intention of the parties:
  Lombard North Central v Butterworth (1988).
  but the use of the word 'condition' is not conclusive:
  Schuler v Wickman (1974).
- by the court:
  Poussard v Spiers & Pond (1876).

A warranty may be identified:
- By statute:
  The Sale of Goods Act 1979.
- By the court:
  Bettini v Guy (1876).

An innominate term will be identified by the fact that it is not a condition or a warranty as above.

An innominate term can generally be breached in different ways with differing results (*Hong Kong Fir Case* (1962)).

The control of exemption clauses

See Chapter 4.

4 Exemption (exclusion or limitation) clauses

ESSENTIALS

You should be familiar with the following areas: ☑

- identification and purposes of exemption clauses
- the need for clauses to be incorporated into a contract
- the interpretation of exemption clauses
- the requirements of The Unfair Contract Terms Act 1977
- the interpretation of 'reasonableness'
- the main provisions of the European Directive on Unfair Terms in Consumer Contracts

Definition

Exemption clauses purport to exclude, wholly or partly, liability for the happening of certain events. A total exclusion is known as an exclusion clause; a partial exclusion is known as a limitation clause.

Exemption clauses are most commonly found in Standard Form Contracts.

There are two views on the function of exemption clauses.

- Such clauses simply define the obligations of the parties.
- Such clauses perform a defensive function. According to this view, one should first construe a contract without regard to the exemption clause, in order to discover the promisor's obligation, and only then consider whether the clauses provide a defence to the breach of such obligations.

The latter is the view traditionally adopted by the courts, who developed a restrictive attitude towards exemption clauses. They did not have the power to hold such clauses invalid on the ground of unreasonability, so they sought to achieve the same end by adopting a restrictive approach towards incorporation and interpretation. They found it difficult, however, to adopt rules which could be applied equally appropriately to both commercial and consumer contracts. This led to the Unfair Contract Terms Act 1977. This Act did not replace the common law rules, but applies jointly alongside those rules.

For an exemption clause to be binding, it must now satisfy:

- The common law rules
(a) It must have been incorporated into the contract.
(b) As a matter of construction it must cover the loss in question.
- The Unfair Contract Terms Act 1977.

Common law requirements

The term must have been incorporated into the contract

This requirement applies to all terms; but has been interpreted strictly in the case of exemption clauses.

Written contracts

Where the contract is signed

The term will automatically have been incorporated. In *L'Estrange v Graucob Ltd* (1934) the plaintiff had bought a slot machine which turned out to be defective. She had signed the contract of sale without reading it. It was held that she was bound by the terms which contained an exemption clause.

Exceptions

Where the offeree has been induced to sign as a result of misrepresentation. In *Curtis v Chemical Cleaning Co Ltd* (1951) the plaintiff had been asked to sign a document headed 'receipt' when she took a dress to be cleaned. On asking why she was required to sign such a document, she was told it was to protect the cleaners in case of damage to the sequins. In fact the clause excluded liability for all damage. The dress was returned badly stained, and the cleaners claimed the protection of the clause. It was held that they were not protected. The extent of the clause had been misrepresented and, therefore, the cleaners could not rely on it.

Where the contract is not signed

Notice by document (ticket cases)

The document must be seen to be a contractual document
In *Chapelton v Barry UDC* (1940) the plaintiff was injured when a deckchair collapsed. The deckchairs were stacked alongside a notice asking the public who wished to use the deck chairs to get tickets and retain them for inspection. On the face of the ticket, there was a large black 3d. On the back were clauses excluding the council from liability for personal injury.

It was held that the defendants could not rely on the exemption clauses as it was not apparent on the face of it that the ticket was a contractual document.

In *Burnett v Westminster Bank* (1966) the plaintiff had accounts at branches A and B of the defendant's bank. A new cheque book for branch A contained a note that, in future, cheques in the book could only be drawn on the account for which they had been prepared. The plaintiff attempted to debit his account in branch B by writing on the cheque as he had been in the habit of doing in the past. The computer failed to recognise the alteration and debited the wrong account. It was held that the statement in the cheque book had not been incorporated into the plaintiff's contract with the bank as it was not clear that the cheque book was a contractual document.

Reasonable notice of the term must be given
In *Parker v SE Railway* (1877) the plaintiff received a ticket which stated on the face 'see back'.

It was held that the plaintiff was bound by an exemption clause printed on the back although he had not read it, because the railway company had given reasonable notice of its existence.

Notice can be reasonable although it refers to other documents. In *Thompson v LMS* (1930) the ticket indicated that the conditions of the contract could be seen at the station masters office, or on the timetable. The exemption clause was in clause 552 of the time-table which cost 6d whilst the ticket itself cost only 2s 6d.

The test is objective, and it is irrelevant that the party affected by the exemption clause is blind or illiterate, or otherwise unable to understand it. But in *Geir v Kujawa* (1970) a notice in English was stuck on the windscreen of a car stating that passengers travelled at their own risk. A German passenger who was known to speak no English was held not to be bound by the clause, as reasonable care had not been taken to bring it to his attention.

Attention must be drawn to any unusual clause

In *Thornton v Shoe Lane Parking* (1971) it was stated that a person who drives his car into a car park might expect to find in his contract a clause excluding liability for loss or damage to the car; but special notice should have been given of a clause purporting to exclude liability for personal injury. In *Interfoto Picture Library Ltd v Stiletto Visual Programmes Ltd* (1989) the Court of Appeal confirmed that onerous conditions required special measures to bring them to the attention of the defendant. The clause in that case was not an exemption clause, but a clause imposing retention charges ten times higher than normal. The Court of Appeal stated, the more unusual the clause, the greater the notice required.

Notice of the term must be communicated to the other party before, or at the time that, the contract is entered into

In *Thornton v Shoe Lane Parking Ltd* (1971) the plaintiff made his contract with the car company when he inserted a coin in the ticket machine. The ticket was issued afterwards, and in any case referred to conditions displayed inside the car park which he could see only after entry.

The rules of offer and acceptance, and the distinctions between offers and invitations to treat must be consulted in order to ascertain when the contract was made. Problems with regard to incorporation can arise in a typical 'battle of the forms' problem (see *Butler Machine Tools Ltd v Excello Corporation* (Chapter 1)).

Notice by display

Notices exhibited in premises seeking to exclude liability for loss or damage, are common, eg 'car parked at owners risk'.

The notice must be seen before, or at the time of entry into contract. In *Olley v Marlborough Court* (1949) Mr and Mrs Olley booked in for a weeks stay at the defendant's hotel. There was a notice on the bedroom which stated 'the proprietors will not hold themselves responsible for articles lost or stolen, unless handed to the manageress for safe-keeping'. Mrs Olley's fur coat was stolen from the bedroom. The Court of Appeal held that the defendants were liable. The plaintiffs saw the notice only after the contract had been entered into; it was therefore not incorporated into the contract.

Notice by a 'course of dealing'
If there has been a course of dealings between the parties, the usual terms may be incorporated into the contract although not specifically drawn to the attention of the parties at the time the contract was entered into.

In *Spurling v Bradshaw* (1956) Bradshaw deposited some orange juice in Spurling's warehouse. The contractual document excluding liability for loss or damage was not sent to Spurling until several days after the contract. It was held that the exclusion clauses were valid since the parties had always done business with each other on this basis.

Note
The transactions must be sufficiently numerous to constitute a course of dealings. The established course of dealings must be consistent. The established course of dealings must not have been deviated from on the occasion in question.

In *Hollier v Rambler Motors* (1972) the Court of Appeal held that bringing a car to be serviced or repaired at a garage on three or four occasions over a period of five years did not establish a course of dealings.

Notice through manifest knowledge
Even though the parties have not dealt with each other in the past, there might be sufficient familiarity with terms which are normal in the trade for contractors involved in that trade.

In *British Crane Hire v Ipswich Plant Hire* (1975) the owner of a crane hired it out to a contractor who was also engaged in the same business. It was held that the hirer was bound by the owner's usual terms though they were not actually communicated at the time of the contract. They were, however, based on a model supplied by a trade association, to which both parties belonged. It was stated that they were reasonable, and were well-known in the trade.

Oral contracts

Whether a clause has been incorporated into an oral contract is a matter of evidence for the court (*McCutcheon v MacBrayn* (1964)).

On a proper construction, the clause covers the loss in question

An exclusion clause is interpreted *contra preferentem*, ie any ambiguity in the clause will be interpreted against the party seeking to rely on it. In *Houghton v Trafalgar Insurance Co Ltd* (1954) it was held that the word 'load' could not refer to people. In *Andrew Bros (Bournemouth) Ltd v Singer & Co Ltd* (1934) an exclusion referring to implied terms was not allowed to cover a term that the car was new since this was an express term.

It was suggested by the House of Lords in *Photo Production Ltd v Securicor Ltd* (1980) that any need for a strained and distorted interpretation of the English language has been banished by the UCTA.

Note
- Especially clear words must be used in order to exclude liability for negligence, eg the use of the word 'negligence', or the phrase 'howsoever caused' (*Smith v South Wales Switchgear Ltd* (1978)). But if these words are not used, provided the wording is wide enough to cover negligence, and there is no other liability to which they can apply then it is assumed that they must have been intended to cover negligence (*Canada Steamship Lines v The King* (1952)). It was stated in *Ailsa Craig Fishing Co Ltd v Malvern Fishing Co Ltd* (1983) that limitation clauses may be interpreted less rigidly than exclusion clauses.
- Only a party to a contract can rely on an exclusion clause (see Chapter 10).
- Especially clear words are required when the breach is of a fundamental nature. In the past, Lord Denning and others argued that it was not possible to exclude breaches of contract which were deemed to be fundamental by any exclusion clause, however widely and clearly drafted (rule of law approach).

However, The House of Lords confirmed in *Photo Production Ltd v Securicor Ltd* (1980) that the doctrine of fundamental breach was a rule of construction not a rule of law, ie liability for a fundamental breach could be excluded if the words were sufficiently clear and precise. The House also stated that:

- The decision in *Harbutts Plasticine Ltd v Wayne Tank Pump Co Ltd* (1970) was not good law. In that case the Court of Appeal had held that as a fundamental breach brought a contract to an end, there was no exclusion clause left to protect the perpetrator of the breach.

- That there is no difference between a 'fundamental term' and a 'condition'.
- A strained construction should not be put on words in an exclusion clause which are clearly and fairly susceptible of only one meaning.
- Where the parties are bargaining on equal terms, they should be free to apportion risks as they wish.
- The courts should be wary of interfering with the settled practices of business men since an exclusion clause often serves to identify who should insure against a particular loss.

The Unfair Contract Terms Act 1977

Some preliminary points to note.

- The title is misleading.
  The Act does not cover all unfair contract terms, only exemption clauses.
  The Act covers certain tortious liability, as well as contractual liability.
- It is important to identify
1 contracts to which the Act applies (s 1 and exceptions)
2 clauses which are void
3 clauses which are subject to the test of 'reasonableness'
- Different sections draw different distinctions.
  In s 2 a distinction is made between personal injury and loss or damage to property.
  In s 3 a distinction is made between consumer and standard form business contracts on one hand, and custom made business contracts on the other hand.
  In ss 4, 5, 6 and 7 a distinction is made between consumer contracts and business contracts.

Content of the Act

Scope
- Section 1
  The act applies to contracts made after 1 February 1978 which arise in the course of business. 'Business' includes a profession and the activities of any government department, and/or public or local authority'. 'Business liability' covers liability:

(a)   from things done in the course of business
(b)   from the occupation of premises used for business purposes.
- Section 5
  Contracts specifically excluded include contracts of insurance, contracts for the transfer of land and international commercial contracts.
- Section 13
  The act limits the effectiveness of clauses that exclude or restrict liability. It also covers clauses which make it difficult to enforce a contract, eg restrictive time limits; or exclude particular remedies. In *Stewart Gill v Horatio Myer & Co Ltd* (1992), it was held that a clause restricting a right of set-off or counter-claim was subject to the Act. It was also held in *Smith v Eric Bush* (1990) that it covered; 'disclaimers which restrictively defined a party's obligation under a contract'. In that case a valuation was stated to be given 'without any acceptance of liability for its accuracy'.

Negligence (s 2)
- An exemption clause or a notice seeking to exclude or restrict liability for death or personal injury caused by negligence is void.
- A clause or notice seeking to exclude or restrict liability for any other loss or damage caused by negligence will be enforced only in so far as it satisfies the requirement of reasonableness.

Negligence means the breach of:

- Any obligation arising from the express or implied terms of a contract to take reasonable care or exercise reasonable skill in the performance of the contract.
- A common law duty to take reasonable care or exercise reasonable skill.
- A common duty of care implied by the Occupiers' Liability Act 1957.

Note
It covers only negligence. It does not cover strict liability.

It is necessary to identify an 'exclusion' of liability, rather than a transfer of liability. In *Phillips Products v Hyland Bros* (1987) the plaintiffs hired an excavator and a driver, under a contract which transferred liability for the negligence of the driver to the hirer. The driver negligently damaged property belonging to the plaintiff. It was held that the clause was an exclusion clause and was subject to UCTA. It was an exclusion clause because it left the plaintiff without anyone to sue.

In *Thompson v T Lohan (Plant Hire) Ltd* (1987) on the other hand, an excavator and driver were hired under the same conditions. The driver negligently killed a third party. It was held by the court that the clause transferring liability to the hirer was not an exclusion clause in this case since the plaintiff was able to sue the hirer. It was merely a clause transferring liability.

Liability arising out of contract (s 3)

Where the transaction is a consumer transaction or a standard form transaction then the party who inserted the clause cannot exclude or restrict his liability for breach of contract, or claim to be entitled to render a contractual performance substantially different from that which was reasonably expected of him, or render no performance at all, unless the exemption clause satisfies the requirement of reasonableness.

A person is a 'consumer' where he does not make or hold himself out as making the contract in the course of business, and the other party does make the contract in the course of business. In contracts for the sale of goods the goods must also be of a type normally sold for private use.

A 'standard form transaction' occurs when the parties deal on the basis of a standard form provided by one of them.

A controversial interpretation of a 'consumer' was made by the Court of Appeal in *R & B Customs Ltd v United Dominion Trust* (1988) where a car was bought by a private company for the business and private use of its directors. It was held by the Court of Appeal that it was not bought 'in the course of a business'. Buying cars was incidental, not central, to the business of the company. If it is incidental only, then the purchase would only be 'in the course of a business' if it was one made with sufficient regularity.

Indemnity clauses (s 4)

Contracts often contain terms requiring one party to indemnify the other against liability incurred by that other in performing the contract. Section 4 makes such a clause void *against a consumer* unless it is reasonable.

Guarantees (s 5)

A manufacturer or distributor cannot, by guarantee, exclude or restrict liability for loss or damage that arises from defects in goods while in *consumer use*, and results from the negligence of a person concerned in the manufacture or distribution of the goods.

Terms implied by The Sale of Goods Act 1979 (s 6)

Liability for breach of the implied term relating to title cannot be excluded or restricted by *any* exemption clause.

The implied terms that goods must correspond with their description; that goods sold in the course of business must be of merchantable quality and fit for any special purpose made known to the seller; that goods must correspond with their sample, cannot be excluded or restricted by a contract term in *a consumer sale*. They can be excluded or restricted, however, in an *inter-business sale*, provided the clause satisfies the test of reasonableness.

Miscellaneous contracts under which the ownership or possession of goods passes, eg contracts of hire, or exchange, or for work and materials (s 7)

A term purporting to exclude or restrict liability in respect of the transfer of ownership or possession will only be effective in so far as it satisfies the test of reasonableness.

An exemption clause purporting to exclude or restrict liability in respect of the goods correspondence with description or sample or their quality or fitness for any particular purpose is of no effect, against a *person dealing as a consumer.*

But as *against a non-consumer,* such a clause will be effective in so far as it satisfies the requirement of reasonableness.

Misrepresentation (s 8)

Terms excluding or restricting liability for misrepresentation are effective only in so far as they satisfy the requirements of reasonableness. This applies to all contracts, not only to contracts which arise in the course of business.

Reasonableness (s 11)

Contract terms are to be adjudged reasonable or not according to the circumstances which were, or ought reasonably to have been known to the parties when the contract was made. Notices not having contractual effect, on the other hand, are to be adjudged on the circumstances obtaining when the liability arose.

Where a person seeks to restrict liability to a specified sum of money, regard should be had to the resources which he could expect to be available to him for the purpose of meeting the liability; and to how far was it open to him to cover himself by *insurance.*

In determining, for the purpose of ss 6 or 7, whether a contract term satisfies the requirement of reasonableness, regard shall be had to the measures specified in Schedule 2.

Schedule 2
- The strength of the bargaining position of the parties relative to each other.
- Whether the customer received an inducement to agree to the term or had an opportunity of entering into a similar contract with other persons but without having to accept similar terms.
- Whether the customer knew, or ought reasonably to have known of the existence and extent of the term.
- Where the exclusion is conditional, whether it was reasonable to expect that compliance with that condition would be practicable.
- Whether the goods were manufactured, processed, or adapted to the special order of the customer.

Interpretation of 'reasonableness'

The burden of proving that a clause is 'reasonable' rests on the person who seeks to rely on it.

Tests
- UCTA s 11 (see above).
- UCTA s 11 Schedule 2. Strictly speaking Schedule 2 only applies to an exclusion of implied terms (ss 6 and 7): in practice the court will probably apply the criteria to other exemption clauses also.
- Decisions of the courts.

Negligence (s 2)
In *Smith v Eric Bush* (1990) and *Harris v Wyre Forest DC* (1990) the House of Lords dealt with two cases involving the validity of an exclusion clause protecting surveyors who had carried out valuations on a house. The House of Lords decided that the clauses were exclusion clauses designed to protect the surveyors against claims for negligence. Lord Griffiths declared that there were four matters which should always be considered:
- Were the parties of equal bargaining power?
- In the case of advice, would it have been reasonable to obtain advice from another source?
- Was the task being undertaken a difficult one, for which the protection of an exclusion clause was necessary?
- What would be the practical consequences for the parties of the decision on reasonableness? For example, would the defendant normally be insured? Would the plaintiff have to bear the cost himself?

In these cases, the House of Lords found that the parties were not of equal bargaining power. Since the houses were at the bottom end of the market it would have been prohibitively expensive to obtain advice from an alternative source; valuing a house was a normal function for a surveyor. Surveyors would normally carry professional liability insurance. The clauses, therefore, did not meet the requirements of reasonability.

Breach of express terms of contract (s 3)

For consumer agreements see *Smith v Eric Bush* (above).

For standard form business agreements see *Photo Production Ltd v Securicor Ltd* (above) where the House of Lords warned against interfering with the settled arrangements of businessmen, and stressed the importance of insurance. See also *Green v Cade Bros* (1983) and *George Mitchell v Finney Lock Seeds* (1983) (below).

Breach of implied terms (ss 6 and 7)

In *Green v Cade Bros* (1978) it was decided that a clause requiring notice of rejection within three days of delivery of seed potatoes was unreasonable since a defect could not have been discovered by inspection within this time. However, a clause limiting damages to the contract price was upheld – as it had been negotiated by organisations representing the buyers and sellers, and 'certified' potatoes had been available for a small extra charge (see Schedule 2 above).

In *George Mitchell v Finney Lock Seeds Ltd* (1983) the buyers suffered losses of £61,000, due to the supply of the wrong variety of cabbage seeds, which were also of inferior quality. The contract limited the liability of the seller to a refund of the price paid (£192). It was held that the clause was not reasonable. Matters taken into consideration were:
* The clause was inserted unilaterally – there was no negotiation.
* Loss was caused by the negligence of the seller.
* The seller could have insured against their liability.
* The sellers implied that they themselves considered the clause unreasonable by admitting that they did not rely on it if they considered a claim to be reasonable.

Misrepresentation (s 8)

In *Cremdean Properties v Nash* (1977) a clause in the special conditions of sale stated that the:

... particulars were believed to be correct, but their accuracy is not guaranteed: Any intending purchaser should satisfy himself by inspection or otherwise as to the correctness of the statements contained in these particulars.

It was held that it was not within a contracting party's power to reclassify a statement as an opinion in order to avoid liability. The clause was an exclusion clause.

In *Collins v Howell Jones* (1980), however, the Court of Appeal held a statement that the:

... vendor does not make or give any representation or warranty and neither the estate agent or any person in their employment has any authority to make or give a representation or warranty whatsoever in relation to the property

This had the effect of defining or limiting the scope of the agents authority.

European Directive on Unfair Terms in Consumer Contracts

This Directive requires the government to bring in legislation to put it into effect as from the 31 December 1994. Draft regulations have been issued (see Revision Notes). In future, exemption clauses, in order to be enforceable, will have to comply with the common law, UCTA, and the new regulations.

The Directive is wider in its effect than UCTA in that it covers all unfair contract terms, not merely exemption clauses, eg harsh terms in banking contracts; the stated exceptions are narrower, eg contracts of insurance and contracts relating to land are not excluded. On the other hand) it is narrower in that it relates only to consumer contracts and only to 'clauses which have not been individually negotiated' (standard form contracts).

A clause will be unfair if 'contrary to the requirements of good faith, it causes a significant imbalance in the parties rights and obligations to the detriment of the consumer'. Unfairness is to be judged by taking into consideration the nature of the goods and services, the circumstances under which the contract was made, and on any other terms of the contract. It is stated that unfairness is not to relate to the definition of the subject matter, or the price. A list of possible unfair terms is given in the annex. Plain English should be used.

If a term is found to be unfair, the term itself will be void, but the rest of the contract may be enforced. The Director General of fair trading may seek an injunction to prohibit the use of unfair terms in individual contracts and in contracts provided by trade associations.

Revision Notes

To be valid an exemption clause must satisfy the tests set by:

The common law
- It must be incorporated into the contract.
- The wording must cover what actually happened.

The Unfair Contract Terms Act 1977

Common law requirements

Incorporation

A term may be incorporated into a contract by being:

Contained in a signed document
L'Estrange v Graucob Ltd (1934)
It will be subject only to defences of:
- Misrepresentation:
  Curtis v Chemical Cleaning Co Ltd (1951).
- *Non est factum*:
  Saunders v Anglia Building Society (1969)
  (Chapter 5).

Contained in an unsigned document
- This must be seen to be a contractual document:
  Chapelton v Barry UDC (1940).
- Reasonable notice of term must be given:
  Parker v SE Railway (1877)
  Thompson v LMS (1930)
  cf *Geir v Kujawa* (1970).
- Attention must be drawn to any unusual clause:
  Thornton v Shoe Lane Parking (1971)
  Interfoto Picture Library Ltd v Stiletto Visual Programmes (1989).
- Communication must be made before or at the time the contract is entered into:
  Thornton v Shoe Lane Parking Ltd (1971).

Displayed in a notice
Olley v Marlborough Court (1949)

Known through a course of dealings
Spurling v Bradshaw (1956)
cf *Hollier v Rambler Motors* (1972)

Known through manifest knowledge
British Crane Hire v Ipswich Plant Hire (1975)

The wording must cover what actually happened

Exemption clauses are construed *contra preferentem*
Andrews Bros v Singer & Co Ltd (1934)
Houghton v Trafalgar Insurance (1954)

Clear explicit words are needed to cover
• Negligence
  eg through the use of the word 'negligence' or the phrase 'howso-ever caused':
  Smith v South Wales Switchgear Motors (1978).
  unless negligence was the only possible ground for liability:
  Hollier v Rambler Motors (1972).
  It was suggested in *Ailsa Craig Fishing v Malvern Fishing* (1983) that the strict rules of interpretation could be relaxed in view of the UCTA 1977.
• Fundamental Breach
  The more fundamental the breach, the clearer and more explicit must be the wording:
  Photo Production v Securicor (1980).

Exemption clauses only protect the parties to the contract
Scruttons Ltd v Midland Silicones Ltd (1962)

However, a second collateral contract was found in *The Eurymedon* (1975) but see *Southern Water Authority v Carey* (1985) and *Norwich City Council v Harvey* (1989).

See Chapter 10 on Agency and Exclusion Clauses.

The Unfair Contract Terms Act 1977

This Act covers contracts arising out of business activities, subject to certain exceptions.

Identification of exemption clauses

The Act covers clauses which exclude or restrict liability or which make enforcement difficult.

It was held to cover restrictions on set-offs and counterclaims in *Stewart Gill v Horatio Myer & Co Ltd* (1992) and disclaimers which defined a party's obligations restrictively in *Smith v Eric Bush* (1990).

Negligence

The Act covers contractual, tortious and statutory negligence. The difference between excluding liability for negligence, and transferring liability for negligence is seen in *Phillips Products v Hyland Bros* (1987) and *Thompson v Lohan (Plant Hire) Ltd* (1987).

Misrepresentation

The difference between excluding liability for misrepresentation, and defining the powers of an agent is seen in *Cremdean Properties v Nash* (1977) and *Collins v Howell Jones* (1980).

Clauses which are void

Exclusions of liability
- For death or personal injury caused by negligence (s 2).
- For loss or damage caused by negligence in a manufacturers guarantee (s 5).
- For implied term re title in any contract (s 6).
- For other terms implied by Sale of Goods Act in consumer contracts (eg correspondence with description; merchantable quality; fitness for purpose).
- For similar terms implied by the Sale and Supply of Goods Act in a consumer contract.

Clauses which are valid only if reasonable

Clauses excluding liability
- For loss or damage to property caused by negligence (s 2).
- For breach of contract in a consumer or standard form contract (s 3).
- For terms implied by the Sale of Goods Act (apart from implied term re title) in an inter business contract (s 6).

- For implied term re title or possession in the Sale and Supply of Goods Act 1973 in all contracts (s 7).
- For other terms implied by The Sale and Supply of Goods Act in inter business contracts (s 7).
- For misrepresentation.

Reasonableness

It is for the defendant to prove that the clause is fair and reasonable. In assessing reasonability, the following matters should be considered:

- Section 11 UCTA
- Schedule 2 UCTA
  which lays down certain criteria for s 6 and s 7.
- Decisions of the courts
  In *Smith v Eric Bush and Harris v Wyre Forest UDC* (1990) the courts stressed the importance of:
  (a) equality of bargaining power;
  (b) availability of alternative source;
  (c) difficulty of the task;
  (d) the practical consequences for the parties.

The courts stressed the relevance of commercial practices in
Photo Production v Securicor (1980)
George Mitchell v Finney Lock Seeds (1983)
Green v Cade Bros (1978).
The availability of insurance seems relevant in all cases.

Consumer

The definition of a consumer is found in s 3 UCTA.
It has been interpreted by the court in a controversial fashion in *R & B Customs Ltd v UDT* (1988).

Draft regulations on unfair contract terms in consumer contracts

A 'business' is defined to include a trade or profession and the activities of any government department or local or public authority. A 'consumer' means a natural person who is acting for purposes outside his business.

Coverage

The regulations will apply to 'any term in a contract concluded between a seller or supplier and a consumer where the term has not been individually negotiated, ie it has been drafted in advance. This will be so even if some other parts of the contract have not been drafted in advance.

The regulations will not apply to contracts which relate to employment; family law or succession rights; companies and partnerships, terms included in order to comply with legislation or an international convention.

Unfairness

A term will be unfair, if contrary to the requirements of good faith it causes a significant imbalance in the parties rights and obligations to the detriment of the consumer. Regard must be had to the nature of the goods and services provided, the other terms of the contract and all the circumstances relating to its conclusion. The definition of the main subject matter and the adequacy of the price or remuneration are not, however, relevant.

In assessing good faith, attention should be paid to:
- the strength of the bargaining positions of the parties;
- whether the consumer had an inducement to agree to the term;
- whether the goods or services were sold or supplied to the special order of the consumer;
- the extent to which the seller or supplier had dealt fairly and equitably with the consumer.

An indicative and non-exhaustive list of terms which may be unfair is included.

The terms should be expressed in plain English, and any ambiguity should be interpreted in the consumers favour.

Effect of an unfair term

- The term itself shall not be binding on the consumer, but the rest of the contract may be enforced.
- The Director General of Fair Trading will have a duty to consider any complaint made to him that a term is unfair. Where appropriate, he must seek an injunction to bar the use of the term not only in

a particular contract, but in similar contracts and also in contracts issued by trade associations.

Note
The regulations are expected to affect mainly contracts issued by banks, finance companies, insurance companies, travel agents, house builders and transport firms.

5 Mistake

ESSENTIALS

You should be familiar with the following areas:	✓
• the classification of mistakes	
• the effect of a common mistake at common law	
• the effect of a mutual mistake at common law	
• the effect of a unilateral mistake at common law	
• 'non est factum'	
• mistakes in equity	

There is much disagreement concerning the effect of mistake on a contract. There are many reasons for this, for example, confusion as to which terms to use; there are a large number of cases which can be interpreted in different ways; there are no recent decisive House of Lords' decisions on the subject; the intervention of equity.

Terminology

The terms used respectively by Cheshire and Anson are as follows:

	CHESHIRE	ANSON	Effect
Same mistake made by both parties	Common mistake	Mutual mistake	May nullify agreement
Parties at cross-purposes	Mutual mistake	Unilateral mistake	Negatives agreement
Parties at cross-purposes, but one party knows that the other is mistaken	Unilateral mistake	Unilateral mistake	Negatives agreement

The terms used by Cheshire are used in this chapter.

Common mistakes

Common mistakes may nullify consent. The parties are agreed, but they are both under the same misapprehension. If this misapprehension is sufficiently fundamental it may nullify the agreement.

At *common law*, this may render the contract void; ie the contract has no legal effect; it is unenforcable by either party and title to property cannot pass under it. The reluctance of the courts to develop the common law doctrine of mistake is probably due to the unfortunate consequences for third parties that can result from holding a contract void.

At *equity* a more flexible approach has developed; contracts containing certain common mistakes have been treated as voidable. In setting aside such contracts the courts have a much wider control over the terms it can impose on the parties.

Common law

In *Bell v Lever Bros Ltd* (1932) Lever Bros agreed to pay two directors of a subsidiary company substantial sums of money in compensation for loss of office, while unaware of the fact that they had engaged in irregular conduct which would have allowed them to be dismissed without pay. The directors themselves had forgotten the incidents and were also unaware that they could be dismissed. There was, therefore, a common mistake as to the validity of the contracts of employment. When Lever Bros discovered the breaches of the service contracts, they asked the court to order the return of compensation paid on the ground that it had been paid as a result of a common mistake. The House of Lords held by a majority of three to two, that the common mistake concerning the validity of the contract of service was not 'sufficiently fundamental' to render the contract void.

Common mistakes 'sufficiently fundamental' to render a contract void

A common mistake as to the existence of the subject matter (res extincta)

In *Galloway v Galloway* (1914) the parties, believing they were married, entered into a separation agreement. Later, they discovered that they were not validly married. It was held that the separation agreement was void for a common mistake.

In *Strickland v Turner* (1852) the court declared void, on the grounds of a common mistake, a contract to purchase an annuity on the life of a person who had already died.

In *Couturier v Hastie* (1856) a buyer bought a cargo of corn which both parties believed to be at sea: the cargo had however, already been disposed of. It was held that the contract was void.

Section 6 Sale of Goods Act 1979 declares that:

Where there is a contract for the sale of specific goods, and the goods without the knowledge of the seller have perished when the contract is made, the contract is void.

However, in *McRae v Commonwealth Disposals Commission* (1951) the commission sold to McRae the right to salvage a tanker lying on a specified reef. There was no such reef of that name, nor was there any tanker. The court found that there was a valid contract and that the commission had impliedly guaranteed the existence of the tanker. The case could be distinguished from the Australian equivalent of s 6 on the ground that there had never been a tanker and it had, therefore, not perished.

Since this case, it has been argued that:

- the word 'mistake' was not mentioned in *Couturier v Hastie* and the case only illustrates that a contract cannot be enforced if there was a failure of consideration. (Atiyah);
- that s 6 of the Sale of Goods Act was based on a misunderstanding of *Couturier v Hastie*;
- that whether a contract is void or valid depends on the construction of the contract, ie even if the subject matter did not exist, the contract will be valid (1) if performance was guaranteed, or (2) if it was the purchase of a 'chance'. Otherwise, the contract would be void (Anson and others).

Mistake as to title (res sua)

In *Cooper v Phibbs* (1867) Cooper, not realising that a fishery already belonged to him, agreed to lease it from Phibbs. It was held that the contract was void.

Mistake as to the possibility of performing the contract

In *Sheik Brothers Ltd v Ochsner* (1957) a contract was held void as the land was not capable of growing the crop contracted for.

In *Griffiths v Brymer* (1903) a contract to hire a room to view the coronation of Edward VI and which was made after the procession had been cancelled was held void (commercial impossibility).

Mistake as to the quality of the subject matter

Lords Atkin and Thankerton both insisted in *Bell v Lever Bros* that to render a contract void, the mistake must go to the 'root of the contract'.

It has been argued that if the mistake in *Bell* was not sufficiently fundamental to render a contract void, then it is highly unlikely that any mistake concerning quality would do so.

Similarly, in *Leaf v International Galleries* (1950) where both parties mistakenly believed that a painting was by Constable, the Court of Appeal stated that the contract was not void for common mistake. In *Solle v Butcher* (1950) the Court of Appeal declined to declare void a lease which both parties believed was not subject to the Rent Acts. A similar stance was taken in in *Grist v Bailey* (1967)) where the parties both believed that a house was subject to a protected tenancy. In *Harrison & Jones Ltd v Bunten & Lancaster* (1953) both parties believed, mistakenly, that Calcutta Kapok was pure Kapok and in *Rose v Pim* (1953) both parties believed that 'horsebeans' were 'feveroles'.

In all these cases the mistakes would seem to be fundamental, but in none of them was the court prepared to hold the contract void. As a result it has been argued by Cheshire, Fifoot and Furmston, amongst others, that a mistake concerning quality will not render a contract void.

However, *Lord Justice Steyn* in *Associated Japanese Bank v Credit du Nord* (1989) stated that not enough attention had been paid to speeches in *Bell v Lever Bros* which did indicate that a narrow range of mistakes in quality could render a contract void, for example, Lord Atkin's statement that 'A contract may be void if the mistake is as to the existence of some quality which makes the thing without that quality essentially different from the thing it was believed to be.' He gave the following example that if a horse believed to be sound turns out to be unsound, then the contract remains valid; but if a horse believed to be a race-horse, turns out to be a cart-horse, then the contract is void.

There are also *obiter dicta* in *Nicholson & Venn v Smith-Marriott* (1947) concerning the provenance of table linen to the effect that a mistake concerning quality can render a contract void.

Glanville Williams has also pointed out that it is not possible to separate a substance from its quality.

There is no metaphysical substance independent of qualities ... qualities considered compositely produce the essence of a substance.

However, in no case since *Bell v Lever Bros* has a contract been found void because of a common mistake concerning the quality of the subject matter.

Equity

Lord Justice Stein in *Associated Japanese Bank v Credit Du Nord* (1989) stated that a court will first examine whether a contract is void at common law. If it is not, then it will examine whether equity will grant rescission. The role of equity according to this view is supplementary, designed to relieve the limitations of the common law.

Rescission on terms was granted by the Court of Appeal in *Solle v Butcher* (1950) where a flat was let in the mistaken belief that it was free from rent control. The court rescinded the lease, but gave the tenant the option of staying there on terms of his paying the extra rent which the landlord could have charged in view of the improvements.

Rescission on terms was also granted in *Grist v Bailey* (1967) where a house was sold in the mistaken belief that it had a protected tenancy and in *Laurence v Lexcourt Holdings* (1978) where there was a common mistake with regard to planning permission.

Rescission without terms was granted in *Magee v Pennine Assurance Co Ltd* (1969) where an agreement by an insurance company to meet a claim was rescinded because the parties were unaware that it was based on a policy which was voidable due to a misrepresentation by the assured.

It has been pointed out, however, that this decision is in direct conflict with the House of Lords' decision in *Bell v Lever Bros* where a contract was held valid despite the parties failing to realise that it was based on a voidable contract of employment. Both cases turned on the mistaken belief that a contract was valid when in fact it was voidable. Lord Atkin also stated in *Bell v Lever Bros* that, 'If mistake operates at all, it operates to negative, or in some cases to nullify consent.' The previous cases could have been distinguished from *Bell* on the ground that they all concerned property. A House of Lords' decision is awaited to clarify the relation between rescission and *Bell v Lever Bros*.

Lord Denning has declared that no common mistake will render a contract *void* but if it concerns a fundamental matter it *will be voidable in equity*. He argues that holding a contract void for a common mistake is unfair to innocent third parties who may be deprived of their rights. He maintains that rescission gives a court a greater degree of flexibility and allows them to protect the rights of innocent third parties.

Lord Denning's view has not met with general approval.

Mutual and unilateral mistakes

These mistakes negative consent, ie prevent the formation of an agreement. The courts adopt an objective test (see Chapter 1) in deciding whether agreement has been reached. It is not enough for one of the parties to allege that he or she was mistaken. Mistake can negative consent in the following cases.

Mutual mistakes concerning the identity of the subject matter

In cases of mutual mistake the parties are at cross-purposes, but there must have been some ambiguity in the situation before the courts will declare the contract void. In *Raffles v Wichelhause* (1864) a consignment of cotton was bought to arrive 'ex *Peerless* from Bombay'. Two ships, both called *Peerless* were due to leave Bombay at around the same time. It was held that there was no agreement since the buyer was thinking of one ship, and the seller was referring to another. Similarly, there was no agreement in *Scriven Bros v Hindley & Co Ltd* (1913) where the seller sold 'tow' and the buyer bought 'hemp'. Again there was an ambiguity as both lots were delivered under the same shipping mark and the catalogue was vague.

But in *Smith v Hughes* (1871) the court refused to declare void an agreement whereby the buyer had thought he was buying old oats when in fact they were new oats, since the contract was for the sale of 'oats' and there was no duty on the seller to disabuse a buyer who was mistaken about the quality of the subject matter.

Unilateral mistake concerning the terms of the contract

Here, one party has taken advantage of the other party's error. In *Hartog v Colin & Shields* (1939) the seller mistakenly offered to sell goods at a given price per pound when they intended to offer them per piece. All the preliminary negotiations had been on the basis of per piece. The buyers must have realised that the sellers had made a mistake. The contract was declared void. In *Smith v Hughes*, however, the contract was for the sale of 'oats' not 'old oats'; it would only have been void if 'old oats' had been a term of the contract.

Unilateral mistake as to the identity of the other party to the contract

There are a number of contradictory cases and theories under this heading. Traditionally, a distinction is made between mistakes as to identity and mistakes as to attributes (eg credit worthiness).

In *Cundy v Lindsay* (1878) a Mr Blenkarn ordered goods from Lindsay signing the letter to give the impression that the order came from Blenkiron & Co, a firm known to Lindsay & Co. He was sent the goods on credit. He resold them to Cundy for cash. It was held that the contract between Lindsay and Blenkarn was void. Lindsay & Co had only intended to do business with Blenkiron & Co. There was, therefore, a mistake concerning the identity of the other party to the contract. The goods, therefore, still belonged to Lindsay & Co.

In *King's Norton Metal Co v Edridge, Merrett & Co Ltd* (1897) on the other hand, a Mr Wallis ordered goods on impressive stationery which indicated that the order had come from Hallam & Co, an old established firm with branches all over the country. The goods were sent on credit and they were resold to Edridge for cash. It was held that the contract between Kings Norton Metal Co and Wallis was not void. The sellers intended to do business with the writer of the letter and they were merely mistaken as to his attributes, ie the size and credit worthiness of his business. The goods, therefore, belonged to Edridge.

In *Boulton v Jones* (1857) the defendant sent an order for some goods to a Mr Brocklehurst, unaware that he had sold the business to his foreman, the plaintiff. The plaintiff supplied the goods but the defendant refused to pay for them as he had only intended to do business with Brocklehurst against whom he had a set-off. Held, there was a mistake concerning the identity of the other party and the contract was therefore void.

From the above three cases, it would seem that a contract is void if the mistaken party intended to do business with another specific person, and the identity of that other person was important to him.

However, the cases all concerned contracts negotiated *at a distance*.

Where the parties are *inter præsentes*, the same rules apply, but there is a presumption that the innocent party intended to do business with the person physically in his presence.

In *Phillips v Brooks* (1919) a jeweller sold a gold ring and delivered it on credit to a customer who had come into his shop and had falsely claimed to be Sir George Bullock a well-known and wealthy man. It was held that the contract was valid. The jeweller had intended to business with the person in his shop.

In *Lewis v Averay* (1972) a rogue claimed to be Richard Green the film actor and produced a pass to Pinewood studios in the name of Richard Green to verify this. He was allowed to drive away a car in return for a cheque and subsequently resold the car for cash to Averay. The cheque bounced, and the seller claimed the return of the car on the ground that he was mistaken as to the identity of the buyer. It was held that the contract was valid; the seller must be presumed to have intended to deal with the person physically in the room with him. Averay kept the car.

There are two cases, however, where the plaintiffs were able to establish a mistake as to the identity of a person in their presence.

In *Ingram v Little* (1961) two sisters sold a car and handed it over against a worthless cheque to a person who claimed to be a Mr Hutchinson of Stanstead House, Caterham. They only did so after one of them had checked that there was a man of that name who lived at that address. The Court of Appeal held the contract void. They considered that the sisters had done enough to establish that they only intended to deal with Mr Hutchinson.

This case has been greatly criticised since it is difficult to reconcile with *Phillips v Brooks* and *Lewis v Averay*.

In *Sowler v Potter* (1940) the lease of a café was granted to Potter who had previously been convicted of keeping a disorderly café under the name of Robinson. The court held that the contract was void because of the lessor's mistaken belief that Potter was not Robinson. This case has also been much criticised and doubted, since it did not seem that Sowler had intended to do business with any other identifiable person. The contract could, in any case, have been set aside for misrepresentation.

Lord Denning maintains that a unilateral mistake concerning the identity of the other party renders a contract voidable not void, as the court may then protect the position of innocent third parties. The contract would, in most cases, be voidable for misrepresentation anyway where one party has misled the other with regard to his identity. The advantage of having the contract declared void for mistake is to avoid the 'bars' to rescission (see Chapter 6).

The Law Reform Committee in 1966 stated that:

... contracts which are at present void because the owner of the goods was deceived or mistaken as to the identity of the person with whom he dealt should in future be treated as voidable and not void so far as third parties are concerned.

Lord Devlin suggested that where two innocent parties are disputing the ownership of an article following a case of mistaken identity, the court should have power to apportion the value of the article between the parties.

Neither suggestion has been implemented by legislation.

Mistake as to the nature of the document signed (defence of *non est factum*)

The scope of this defence has been limited since the decision in *Saunders v Anglia Building Society (Gallie v Lee)* (1971) where an old lady was persuaded by her nephew to sign a document conveying her house to her nephew's friend. She had believed that she was signing a deed of gift to her nephew. She had not read the document because her glasses were broken. It was held that the document was valid. Before it will be set aside:

- The signed document must be fundamentally different in effect from what it was thought to be.
- The signatory must prove that he or she had not been negligent in signing the document.

It is also thought that it will only protect a person who is under some disability. The defence did succeed in *Lloyds Bank plc v Waterhouse* (1990) where the defendant who was illiterate signed a guarantee of his son's debt to the bank. The father thought that the guarantee covered the purchase price of a farm, but in fact it covered all his son's indebtedness to the bank. It was held that the effect of the document was fundamentally different from what it was believed to be and there was no negligence. The contract was therefore void.

In *UDT Ltd v Western* (1976) it was held that these same rules applied to cases where a person had signed a form before all the details required by the form had been entered.

Mistake in equity

The narrow approach taken by the common law towards mistake is supplemented by the more flexible approach of equity. The following remedies may be available.

Rescission

See common mistake (above).

Rectification

Where there has been a mistake, not in the actual agreement but in reducing it to writing, equity will order rectification of the document so that it coincides with the true agreement of the parties.

Necessary conditions

1. The document does not represent the intention of *both* parties, or one party mistakenly believed a term was included in the document and the other party *knew* of this error. In *Roberts & Co Ltd v Leicester CC* (1961) the completion date of a contract was rectified at the request of one party, because it was clear that the other party was aware of the error when the contract was signed.

   If the document fails to mention a term which one party, but not the other, had intended to be a term of the contract, there is no case for rectification.

2. There must have been a *concluded* agreement, but not necessarily a legally enforceable contract. In *Joscelyne v Nissen* (1970) a father and daughter agreed that the daughter should take over the car-hire business. In return, the father would continue to live in the house and the daughter would pay all the household expenses. This last provision was not included in the written contract. It was held that the contract should be rectified to include it.

   Note

   A document which accurately records a prior agreement cannot be rectified because the agreement was made under some mistake (*Rose v Pim* above). Equity rectifies documents not agreements.

Rectification is an equitable remedy and is available at the discretion of the court. Lapse of time or third party rights may prevent rectification.

Refusal of specific performance

Specific performance will be refused when the contract is void at common law. Equity may also refuse specific performance where a contract is valid at law, but only 'where a hardship amounting to injustice would have been inflicted upon him by holding him to his bargain'.

In *Webster v Cecil* (1861) the defendant, having previously refused the plaintiff's offer of £2,000 for his land, wrote to the plaintiff offering to sell it to him for £1,250 instead of £2,250 as he had intended. The plaintiff accepted the offer. Specific performance was refused since the plaintiff must have been aware of the error (unilateral mistake).

Where there is no blame on the plaintiff the situation is more difficult. In *Malins v Freeman* (1837) the defendant had mistakenly bought the wrong property at an auction. Specific performance was refused. In *Tamplin v James* (1880), however, the court ordered specific performance where the defendant had bid for a property under an error as to its true extent. Presumably, being forced to buy a totally different property from the one he intended would have caused greater hardship than being forced to buy a property whose dimensions differed from his expectations.

Revision Notes

Effect of a mistake at common law

The general rule is that a mistake has no effect on a contract, but certain mistakes of a fundamental nature, sometimes called operative mistakes, may render a contract void.

Mistakes which may render a contract void

If the contract is rendered void, then the parties will be returned to their original positions, and this may defeat the rights of innocent third parties who may have acquired an interest in the contract.

Common mistakes (ie both parties make the same mistake)

If a common mistake renders the contract void, it is said to nullify the agreement, ie agreement was reached but it has no effect.

In *Bell v Lever Bros* (1932) it was stated that to nullify the agreement, the 'mistake must go to the root of the contract'.

Common mistakes concerning the existence of the subject matter of the contract (*res extincta*)
Galloway v Galloway (1914)
Strickland v Turner (1852)
Couturier v Hastie (1856)
Sale of Goods Act 1979, s 6.

But see
McRae v Commonwealth Disposals Commission (1951) where the Australian court held that the defendants had impliedly guaranteed the existence of the wreck.

Common mistakes as to title ie the thing sold already belongs to the buyer (*res sua*)
Cooper v Phibbs (1867)

Common mistakes concerning the possibility of performance
- Physical impossibility:
  Sheik Brothers v Ochsner (1957).
- Commercial impossibility:
  Griffiths v Brymer (1903).

Common mistake concerning the quality of the subject matter
Cheshire, Fifoot and Furmston argue that a mistake concerning quality will never render a contract void, and cite:
Bell v Lever Bros (1932)
Leaf v International Galleries (1950)
Solle v Butcher (1950).

But Lord Justice Steyn in *Associated Japanese Bank v Credit du Nord* (1988) claimed that a sufficiently fundamental mistake concerning quality would render a contract void ie where the quality concerned identified the subject matter.

Lord Justice Steyn has also stated that the court must first investigate whether the common mistake renders the contract void at common law. If not, it must then investigate whether it is voidable in equity (see below).

Mutual mistakes (ie the parties are at cross-purposes)

An operative mutual mistake negatives agreement, ie agreement has not been reached.

Mutual mistake concerning the identity of the subject matter will render a contract void, provided there is some ambiguity in the agreement. The test is an objective one:
Raffles v Wichelhause (1864)
Scriven Bros v Hindley (1913)
cf *Smith v Hughes* (1871).

Unilateral mistakes (one party is aware of the other's mistake)

An operative unilateral mistake also negatives agreement.
- A unilateral mistake concerning the terms of the contract will render a contract void, provided that the mistake was serious:
  Hartog v Colin & Shields (1939)
  cf *Smith v Hughes* (1871).
- A unilateral mistake as to the identity of the other party to the contract will render a contract void, provided the mistaken party

intended to deal with another specific person whose identity was important to him.
* There must be a mistake as to identity, not as to attributes:
  Cundy v Lindsay (1878)
  Kings Norton Metal Co v Edridge (1872)
  Boulton v Jones (1857).
  But see
  Sowler v Potter (1940).
* Where the parties are *inter præsentes* there is a presumption that a party intended to deal with the person physically in his presence:
  Phillips v Brooks (1919)
  Lewis v Averay (1972).
  But see
  Ingram v Little (1961)
  Sowler v Potter (1940).
* Unilateral mistake as the effect of a document signed:
  Saunders v Anglia Building Society (1971).
  The mistaken person must prove that the document was radically different in effect from what he thought it to be and that he was not negligent in signing the document.

Mistake in equity

Rescission

If a common mistake does not render a contract void at common law then the court will examine whether it is voidable in equity. If the mistake is of a fundamental nature, the court may grant rescission on terms:
Solle v Butcher (1950)
Grist v Bailey (1967)
Laurence v Lexcourt Holdings (1978)
Magee v Pennine Insurance Company Ltd (1969).
But it is argued that the decision in *Magee* conflicts with the House of Lords decision in *Bell v Lever Bros* (1932).

Note
The same bars to rescission apply to rescission for common mistake as apply to rescission for misrepresentation. See Chapter 6.

Rectification

A document may be rectified if it does not accurately reflect the agreement, provided:
* it fails to reflect the intention of both parties;
* there was a concluded agreement:
  Roberts & Co Ltd v Leicester CC (1961)
  Joscelyne v Nissan (1970).

Refusal of specific performance

Specific performance may be refused where to enforce the contract would cause hardship amounting to injustice:
Webster v Cecil (1861)
Malins v Freeman (1837)
Tamplin v James (1880).

6 Misrepresentation, duress, and undue influence

ESSENTIALS

You should be familiar with the following areas:	✓
• the requirements of misrepresentation	
• the effect of misrepresentation	
• the requirements of economic duress	
• the classifications of undue influence	
• the effect of undue influence on third parties	

Misrepresentation

It is not only a breach of the terms of a contract which can give rise to legal action. If a statement made to induce the contract, but which does not become a term of the contract turns out to be untrue, then the misled party may be able to rescind the contract or sue for damages.

Representations and terms of a contract

Material statements made during negotiations leading to a contact may be either:

- Statements which form the express terms of the contract.
  If these are untrue, the untruth constitutes a breach of contract.
- Statements which do not form part of the contract but which helped to induce the contract.
  Such statements are called 'mere representations'. If untrue, they are 'misrepresentations'.

Now that damages can be awarded for negligent misrepresentations, the distinction has lost much of its former significance. However, the rules with regard to remoteness and assessment of damages differ according to whether the action is for breach or for misrepresentation so the distinction can still have some importance.

(For the distinction between terms and 'mere representations', see Chapter 3.)

In a question on misrepresentation, it is necessary to identify the misrepresentation, and the appropriate remedy or remedies.

In particular, the interpretation of the Misrepresentation Act in *Royscot Trust Ltd v Rogerson* (1991) has recently been the subject of much attention.

Requirements of misrepresentation

Definition: An untrue statement of fact made by one party to the contract (representor) to the other (representee) which induces the other to enter into the contract.
It must be:

A statement of fact

- Not a mere 'puff', ie a statement so vague as to be without effect, eg describing a house as a 'desirable residence'.
- Not a promise. A promise to do something in the future is only actionable if the promise amounted to a binding contract (*Kleinwort Benson Ltd v Malaysian Mining Corp Bhd* (1989)).
- Not a statement of opinion, eg in *Bisset v Wilkinson* (1927) the vendor of a farm which had never been used as a sheep farm stated that in his judgment the farm would support 2,000 sheep. It was held to be a statement of opinion.

But a statement expressed as an opinion may be treated as a statement of fact if the person making the statement was in a position to know the true facts. In *Smith v Land & House Properties Corp* (1884) the vendor of a hotel described it as 'let to a most desirable tenant', when the tenant had for a long time been in arrears with the rent. The Court of Appeal held there was a misrepresentation of fact.

In *Esso Petroleum Ltd v Mardon* (1976) Esso informed the prospective tenant of a petrol station that the throughput in the station would be approximately 200,000 gallons a year. Esso argued that this was a statement of opinion. The case was, however, distinguished from *Bisset* on the ground that Esso had special knowledge and skill in the forecasting of throughputs, and the statement was, therefore, one made by an expert, with the intention that it should be relied on.

- Not a statement of intention. But if the representor did not have that intention, then it is a misstatement of fact as in *Edgington v Fitzmaurice* (1885) where the directors issued a prospectus claiming that the money raised was to be used to improve the company's buildings and to expand its business. Their real intention was to pay off the company's debts. This was held fraudulent misrepresentation.
- Not a statement of law
  The distinction, again, between law and fact is not always clear.

Suggested distinctions:
Content and meaning of a public Act of Parliament = law
Content of a private Act or document = fact
Meaning of a private act or document = law.
A statement may contain a misrepresentation of law and fact, in which case it seems that the availability of relief will depend on which part of the statement provided the major inducement to contract.

An active representation

The statement will normally be in words, but other forms of communication which misrepresent the facts will suffice, as in *Horsefall v Thomas* (1862) (below).

Failure to make a statement, however, will not generally qualify as misrepresentation.

Exceptions
- Where facts have been selected to give a misleading impression eg in one case the court stated that if a vendor of land states that farms are let, but omits to say that the tenants have been given notice to quit, his statement will be a misrepresentation of fact (*Dimmock v Hallett* (1866)).
- Change of circumstance
  Where circumstances have changed since a representation was made, then the representor has a duty to correct the statement. In *With v O'Flanagan* (1936) it was stated that a medical practice was worth £2,000 a year. This was accurate when made, but later the doctor became ill, and by the time the practice changed hands, it was practically worthless. It was held that there was a duty to disclose the changed circumstances.
- Contracts *uberrimae fideii* (of the utmost good faith)

(a) Contract of insurance. Material facts must be disclosed, ie facts which would influence an insurer in deciding whether to accept the proposal, or to fix the amount of the premium, eg a policy of life insurance has been avoided because it was not disclosed that the proposer had already been turned down by other insurers.

(b) Family arrangements, eg a re-settlement of land, an agreement to abide by the terms of a will that has not been properly executed. In *Gordon v Gordon* (1821), a division of property made on the basis that the elder son was illegitimate was set aside upon proof that the younger son had concealed his knowledge of a private marriage ceremony solemnised before the birth of his brother.

(c) Analogous contracts where there is a duty to disclose, not material, but unusual facts - eg contracts of suretyship.

It must have been a material inducement

For instance, it must be on a matter which would affect the decision of a reasonable man as to whether or on what terms he would be prepared to enter into the contract.

A statement likely to induce a person to contract will normally be assumed to have done so.

Exceptions

- Where the misrepresentee or his agent actually knew the truth.
- Where the misrepresentee was ignorant of the misrepresentation when the contract was made. In *Horsfall v Thomas* (1862) the vendor of a gun concealed a defect in the gun. (Misrepresentation by conduct.) The buyer, however, bought the gun without examining it. It was held that this was not actionable misrepresentation.
- If the misrepresentee did not allow the representation to affect his judgment. In *Attwood v Small* (1838) the owner offered to sell a mine and made exaggerated statements as to its capacity. The buyer appointed agents to investigate, and they reported that the statements were true. It was held that this was not actionable misrepresentation. The buyer had relied on his own agent's statements. Provided that the representation was one of the inducements, it need not be the sole inducement. The fact that the representee did not take advantage of an opportunity to check the statement is no bar to an action for misrepresentation. In *Redgrave v Hurd* (1881) a solicitor was induced to purchase a house and practice by the innocent misrepresentation of the seller. It was held that he was entitled to rescission although he did not examine the documents which

were available to him and which would have indicated to him the true state of affairs.

It was held in *Gran Gelato v Richcliff* (1992) that relying on the misrepresentation without checking it did not amount to contributory negligence.

Effect of misrepresentation

Misrepresentation renders a contract *voidable* (not *void*).

The remedies for misrepresentation are:

- Affirmation
  The misled party may, if it wishes, affirm the contract.
- Avoidance of contract
  Where the misled party has not performed the contract, he may refuse to perform and rely on the misrepresentation as a defence.
- Rescission
  The misled party may rescind the contract by:
  (a) informing the other party; or
  (b) where a fraudulent party cannot be traced, by informing the police (*Car & Universal Finance Co Ltd v Caldwell* (1965)); or
  (c) bringing legal proceedings.

Rescission normally means restoring the parties as far as is possible to the position they were in before they entered into the contract.

But in *Cheese v Thomas* (1993) the court declared that the court must look at all the circumstances to do what was 'fair and just'. In that case a house which had been jointly bought had to be sold afterwards at a considerable loss. The agreement between the two parties for the purchase of the house was rescinded, but the court held that it was not necessary for the guilty party to bear the whole of the loss. It was just that the proceeds should be divided according to their respective contributions. This contrasts with the normal situation where a property has diminished in value, and the misled party would get all his money returned (*Erlanger v New Sombrero Phosphate Co Ltd*). As part of this restoration, equity may order a sum of money to be paid to the misled person to *indemnify* him or her against *any obligations necessarily created by the contract.*

In *Whittington v Seale-Hayne* (1900) the plaintiffs, breeders of prize poultry, were induced to take a lease of the defendant's premises by his innocent misrepresentation that the premises were in a sanitary condition. Under the lease, the plaintiffs covenanted to execute all works required by any local or public authority. Owing to the insanitary conditions of the premises, the water supply was poisoned, the plaintiffs' manager and his family became very ill, and the poultry became valueless for breeding purposes, or died. In addition, the local authority required the drains to be renewed. The plaintiffs sought an indemnity for all their losses. The court rescinded the lease, and held that the plaintiffs could recover an indemnity for what they had spent on rates, rent and repairs under the covenants in the lease, because these expenses arose necessarily out of the contract. It refused to award compensation for other losses, since to do so would be to award damages, not an indemnity, there being no obligation created by the contract to carry on a poultry farm on the premises or to employ a manager etc.

Note

Rescission, even if enforced by the court, is always the act of the defrauded party. It is effective from the date it is communicated to the representor or the police (see above) and not from the date of any judgment in subsequent litigation.

Rescission is available for every kind of misrepresentation, but is subject to certain bars.

Limits to the right of rescission

Affirmation of the contract

The representee may not rescind if he has affirmed the contract after learning of the misrepresentation either by declaring his intention to proceed with the contract or by performing some act from which such an intention can be inferred. In *Long v Lloyd* (1958) the buyer of a lorry undertook a long journey after discovering serious defects in the lorry. It was held that he had affirmed the contract.

Lapse of time

This can provide evidence of affirmation where the misrepresentee fails to rescind for a considerable time after discovering the falsity.

In cases of *innocent* misrepresentation lapse of time can operate as a separate bar to rescission. In *Leaf v International Galleries* (1950) the plaintiff bought a picture which the seller had innocently misrepresented to be by Constable. Five years later the plaintiff discovered it was not by Constable and immediately sought to rescind the contract. It was held to be barred from doing so by lapse of time.

Restitution must be possible

A person seeking to rescind the contract must be able and willing to restore what he has received under it. However, rescission is an equitable remedy, and the court will not allow minor failures in the restoration to the original position to stand in the way. In *Erlanger v New Sombrero Phosphate Co Ltd* (1878) the purchaser had worked phosphate mines briefly. It was held that he could rescind by restoring property and accounting for any profit derived from it.

Third party rights

There can be no rescission if third parties have acquired rights in the subject matter of the contract (*Phillips v Brooks* (1919) and *Lewis v Avery* (1973) (see Chapter 5)). However, in *Car & Universal Finance Co Ltd v Caldwell* rescission was not barred because it occurred before the intervention of a bona fide purchaser for value.

Effect of Misrepresentation Act 1967

Before 1967, where a misrepresentation had been incorporated into the contract as a term of the contract, rescission could not be obtained, and contracts for the sale of land, or the sale of shares could not be rescinded once they had been 'executed'. These bars have been removed by s 1 Misrepresentation Act 1967.

Section 2 Misrepresentation Act 1967 confers on the court a discretion to award damages 'in lieu of rescission' in cases of innocent misrepresentation. There has been much discussion as to whether damages 'in lieu' can be awarded where rescission is no longer available (see bars above). In *Alton Garages (Bromley) Ltd v Monk* (1981) it was held that damages could not be awarded when the right to rescission had been lost.

Damages

There are five ways in which damages may be claimed for misrepresentation. It seems likely that, in future, damages will generally be claimed under the Misrepresentation Act 1967; but there are still cases where damages can only be claimed if at all, at common law, or common law claims are more beneficial.

Note

Rescission and damages are alternative remedies in many cases, but if the victim of *fraudulent* or *negligent* misrepresentation has suffered consequential loss he may rescind and sue for damages.

Damages can be claimed on different bases, according to the kind of misrepresentation that was committed.

Damages in the tort of deceit for fraudulent misrepresentation
It is up to the misled party to prove that the misrepresentation was made:
- fraudulently, ie knowingly, without belief in its truth; or
- recklessly ie, careless as to whether it be true or false (*Derry v Peek* (1889)).

The burden of proof on the misled party is a heavy one.

Damages in the tort on negligence
Victims of negligent misrepresentation may be able to sue under *Hedley Byrne v Heller & Partners* (1964). The misrepresentee must prove (i) that the misrepresentor owed him a duty to take reasonable care in making the representation, ie there must be a 'special relationship'; (ii) the statement had been made negligently.

Damages under s 2(1) Misrepresentation Act 1967
Section 2(1) Misrepresentation Act 1967 provides that:

Where a person has entered into a contract after a misrepresentation has been made to him by another party thereto, and as a result of it has suffered loss, then if the misrepresentor would be liable for damages if it had been made fraudulently, he will be so liable notwithstanding that the misrepresentation was not made fraudulently, unless he proves that he had reasonable grounds to believe, and did believe up to the time the contract was made that the facts represented were true.

Note
This is a more beneficial remedy for the misrepresentee as he or she only need prove that the statement is untrue. It is for the misrepresentor to prove that there were good grounds for making the statement, and the burden of proof is a heavy one. In *Howard Marine & Dredging Co Ltd v Ogden* (1978) the owner of two barges told the hirer that the capacity of the barges was 1,600 tons. He obtained these figures from the Lloyds list, but in this case the Lloyds list was incorrect. The court held that he did not have good grounds for this statement. He should have consulted the manufacturer's specifications which should have been in his possession.

Assessment of damages
Damages in the tort of deceit and the tort of negligence are assessed on the tortious basis of reliance, ie the plaintiff is entitled to be put in the

position he was in before the tort was committed, as contrasted with the normal contractual basis for assessing damages, ie the expectations basis – to put the plaintiff in the position he would have been in had the contract been performed.

Controversy raged for many years as to whether the tortious basis or the contractual basis should be used under s 1(2) Misrepresentation Act 1967. It has now been confirmed by the Court of Appeal in *Royscot v Rogerson* (1991) that because of the actual wording of the act with its 'fiction of fraud', damages should be awarded on a reliance basis as in the tort of fraud. It was also held in that case, again because of the 'fiction of fraud' that the rules of remoteness which apply only to the tort of deceit should be applied, ie damages would be awarded to cover all losses which flow directly from the untrue statement, whether or not those losses were foreseeable. (In contract and in all torts other than deceit, the losses must be foreseeable.)

In *Royscot Trust v Rogerson* (1991) a customer arranged to acquire a car on hire-purchase from a car dealer. The finance was to be provided by a finance company, the Royscot Trust, which insisted on a deposit of 20%. The dealer falsified the figures in order to indicate a deposit of 20% as required. Some months later, the customer wrongfully sold the car, thus depriving the finance company of its property. The finance company sued the dealer under s 1(2) Misrepresentation Act. It was held by the Court of Appeal that the finance company could recover damages from the car dealer to cover the loss of the car, since the loss followed the misrepresentation, the remoteness rules applicable to the tort of deceit would be applied and the loss did not need to be foreseeable.

Controversy has followed this decision, since the tort of deceit to which this rule only previously applied is difficult to establish and involves moral culpability on the part of the defendant. It has now been extended to an action which is relatively easy to establish (see *Howard Marine and Dredging v Ogden*) and may only involve carelessness.

Further problems are caused by the decision of the Court of Appeal in *East v Maurer* (1991), a case in the tort of deceit where it was held that 'all damages flowing directly from the fraud' would cover damages for loss of profit – a heading previously considered to be appropriate only to expectation damages in contract. It is a matter for speculation whether the courts will apply this decision to cases under the Misrepresentation Act and cover loss of profit under the heading of reliance loss on the basis that all losses which flow directly from the misrepresentation will be recoverable.

A generous interpretation of s 1(2) Misrepresentation Act 1967 had also been applied by the court in *Naughton v O'Callaghan* (1990) where reliance damages had been awarded to cover not only the difference between the value of the colt and the value it would have had if the statements made about it were correct (the *prima facie* rule); but also the cost of its maintenance since the sale.

It has been alleged that these three cases swell the amount of damages which can be awarded under the Misrepresentation Act to a greater extent than that intended by Parliament, and that the damages available for misrepresentation can now exceed those available for breach of contract.

Damages for wholly innocent misrepresentation

Damages cannot be claimed for a misrepresentation which is not fraudulent or negligent, but:

• An indemnity may be awarded (see above).
• Damages in lieu of rescission may be awarded under the Misrepresentation Act 1967 (see above). It is not clear what the measure of damages would be under s 2(2). It has been suggested that the damages would represent the difference in value, but that no consequential losses would be covered.

Damages for breach of contract

Where the misrepresentation has become a term of the contract, the misrepresentee can sue for damages for breach of contract.

Duress

Duress renders a contract voidable. Rescission will normally be sought from the courts. See above for bars to rescission. In *North Ocean Shipping Co Ltd v Hyundai Construction Co Ltd (The Atlantic Baron)* (1979) the court found economic duress but refused rescission on the ground that the plaintiff had affirmed the contract.

Duress involves coercion.

Duress to the person

This requires actual or threatened violence to the person. Originally, it was the only form of duress recognised by the law.

Duress to goods

Threat of damage to goods. Traditionally this has not been recognised by the law, but in view of the development of economic duress, it is assumed that duress to goods would today be a ground for relief.

Economic duress

Illegitimate commercial pressure. This was discussed by the court in the *Siboen & Sibotre* (1976); recognised by the court but not remedied in the *Atlantic Baron* (above); applied by the House of Lords in *Universe Tankships Ltd of Monrovia v ITWF* (1983) where the union had 'blacked' a tanker, and refused to let it leave port until certain moneys had been paid. The court considered that this amounted to economic duress and ordered return of the money. It was stated that economic duress requires:

- 'Compulsion or coercion of the will'
  It was originally suggested that this involved a lack of consent; but it has been pointed out by Professor Atiyah that duress actually involves positively and consciously choosing between two evils.
  In *Pao On v Lau Yiu Long* (1980) Lord Scarman listed the following indications of compulsion or coercion of the will.
  1. Did the party coerced have an alternative course open to him?
  2. Did the party coerced protest?
  3. Did the party coerced have independent advice?
  4. Did the party take steps to avoid the contract?
- Illegitimate pressure
Normal commercial pressure is not sufficient; there must be some element of illegitimacy in the pressure exerted, eg a threatened breach of contract. Economic duress is often pleaded together with lack of consideration in cases where a breach of contract is threatened by the promisor, unless he receives additional payment.

In *Atlas Express Co v Kafco Ltd* (1989), Kafco a small company which imported and distributed basketware, had a contract to supply Woolworths. They contracted with Atlas for delivery of the basketware to Woolworths. The contract commenced, then Atlas discovered they had underpriced the contract, and told Kafco that unless they paid a minimum sum for each consignment, they would cease to deliver. Kafco were heavily dependant on the Woolworths contract, and knew that a failure to deliver would lead both to the loss of the contract and an action for damages. At that time of the year, they could not find an alternative carrier, and agreed, under protest, to make the extra payments. Atlas sued for Kafko's non-payment. It was held that the agreement was invalid for economic duress and also for lack of consideration.

Cf *Williams v Roffey Bros & Nicholls* (1991) (Chapter 2).

Note

Not all threatened breaches of contract will amount to economic duress. It will only be the case when the threatened party has no reasonable alternative open to him (see 1 above). The normal response to a breach of contract is to sue for damages.

The following threats are not illegitimate:

- a threat not to enter into a contract;
- a threat to institute civil proceedings;
- a threat to call the police.

The conditions necessary for economic duress are still not totally clear. Because of the vagueness of the phrase 'coercion of the will', emphasis has switched to the illegitimacy of the threat, but even here there is a lack of a comprehensive explanation of those threats that are to be deemed illegitimate.

Undue influence

Pressure not amounting to duress at common law, whereby a party is excluded from the exercise of free and independent judgment.

Undue influence is based on the misuse of a relationship of trust or confidence between the parties. Where found, it renders a contract voidable. The innocent party will need to apply to the court for rescission of the contract. For the bars to rescission, see 'Misrepresentation'.

There are two separate sets of circumstances which will amount to undue influence.

Contracts where undue influence is presumed

These are contracts between:

- parent and child
- trustee and beneficiary
- solicitor and client
- doctor and patient
- religious adviser and disciple

It was confirmed in *Barclays Bank v O'Brien* (1993) that undue influence may also be presumed from a long relationship of confidence and trust between the parties, eg between husband and wife or where one party had been accustomed to rely for guidance and advice on the other, as in *Lloyds Bank v Bundy* (1975) where Mr Bundy, an elderly west country farmer, on the advice of the local Lloyds Bank assistant manager, granted a charge to the bank over the family farm, to guarantee his sons indebtedness to the bank. Mr Bundy had all his life relied on Lloyds Bank for financial advice. The court set aside the charge on the ground of undue influence on the part of the bank.

Note
A bank does not incur undue influence in normal circumstances. In *National Westminster Bank v Morgan* (1985) the court held that the normal commercial relationship of banker and customer had not been displaced.

Before a transaction can be set aside for presumed undue influence, it must be *manifestly disadvantageous* to the person seeking to avoid the contract.

The stronger party can disprove undue influence by showing that:

- full disclosure of all material facts was made;
- the consideration was adequate;
- the weaker party was in receipt of independent legal advice.

Contracts where undue influence has to be proved

The burden of proof lies on the plaintiff to show that such influence did exist and was exerted.

It was confirmed in *CIBC Mortgages v Pitt* (1993) that the transaction does not have to be *manifestly disadvantageous* in the case of actual undue influence.

Effect of undue influence on a third party

In *Barclays Bank v O'Brien* (1993) Mrs O'Brien had signed a guarantee which used the jointly owned matrimonial home as security for a loan made to her husband's business. Her husband had told her it was for a maximum of £60,000, but in fact it was for £130,000. Mrs O'Brien had not read the guarantee when she signed it and had not been advised by the bank to consult an independent solicitor. The House of Lords held that there was no undue influence in this case, but there was misrepresentation on the part of the husband. They further held that where there was undue influence or misrepresentation or other legal wrong then the injured party's right to have the transaction set aside would be enforceable against the third party provided the third party had actual or constructive notice of the wrong. Such notice would arise where:

- the parties were in an emotional relationship, eg co-habitees (heterosexual or homosexual) or child and aged parents;
- one party was undertaking a financial liability on behalf of the other which was not to his or her advantage.

The court also held that in the above situation the third party could discharge his duty making clear to the party concerned the full nature of the risk he or she is taking on, eg:

- by conducting a personal interview; and
- urging independent advice.

This doctrine of constructive notice applies to sureties (guarantors) but does not apply where a bank makes a joint loan to both parties as the facts in that situation do not meet the requirements set out in *Barclays Bank v O'Brien*. See *CIBC Mortgages v Pitt* (1993).

A bank, or other financial institution, may therefore have a guarantee or mortgage set aside for undue influence:

- where the bank itself has exercised undue influence (*Lloyds Bank v Bundy*) (above);
- where the person exercising undue influence was acting as an agent of the bank. In *Avon Finance v Bridger* (1985) the finance company gave Bridger the mortgage documents so that he could obtain his parents' signature. Held he was an agent for the company and his undue influence would also be that of the company's;
- where it has constructive or actual notice that there is a possibility of undue influence as explained in *Barclays Bank v O'Brien* (above).

Inequality of bargaining power/unfairness/ unconscionability

Lord Denning stated in *Lloyds Bank v Bundy*:

The English law gives relief to one who, without independent advice, enters into a contract upon terms that are very unfair, or transfers property for a consideration which is grossly inadequate when his bargaining power is impaired.

Other judges, however, based their decision on undue influence.
Lord Denning has repeated his views in other cases, claiming that the law recognised a principle of 'inequality of bargaining power or unfairness'.
He has cited in support of his views:

Lloyds Bank v Bundy (above)
D & C Builders v Rees (Chapter 2)
Schroeder Music Publishing v Macaulay (Chapter 7)
Doctrine of economic duress (above)

Others have argued that courts are not prepared to intervene purely on the grounds of unfairness or inequality in bargaining power. Before the courts will intervene, the contract must fall into one of the following categories.

Special type – where inequality of bargaining power is a relevant issue in considering the validity of the contract

For example, contracts in restraint of trade.
In *Schroeder Music Publishing Co Ltd v Macaulay* (1974), inequality of bargaining power was taken into consideration in deciding whether the restraint was reasonable. However, in *Alec Lobb v Total Oil* (1985) it was held that inequality of bargaining power by itself was not enough – the restraint must also be oppressive and unconscionable.

A particular kind of exemption clause

See Chapter 4 for the clauses required by UCTA to be reasonable and the criteria for assessing reasonability.

Recognised misconduct on the part of the advantaged party that would justify the court intervening

For example:
- duress (see above);
- undue influence (see above);
- unconscionable bargains.

Equity can give relief against 'unconscionable bargains' in cases where one party is in a position to exploit the weakness of the other. Traditionally, however, this jurisdiction has been restricted to 'ignorant persons' and 'expectant heirs'.
Lord Scarman in *Pao On v Lau Yiu Long* (above) rejected inequality of bargaining power as a ground for invalidity. 'This as a ground of invalidity distinct from duress would be unhelpful because it would render the law uncertain.'

The statement by Lord Denning concerning a general doctrine of inequality of bargaining powers was also given short shrift by the House of Lords in *National Westminster Bank v Morgan* (above). The statement was described as too wide.

Given the flexibility of the some of the above rules, however, it has been suggested that although the bases may vary, the effect is not very different from Lord Denning's proposition.

Revision Notes

Misrepresentation

An 'actionable misrepresentation' is an untrue statement of fact, made by one party to the contract to the other party, and which induces the other party to enter into the contract.

Requirements of misrepresentation

It must be a statement of fact
A statement of fact is not:
* a mere puff;
* a promise
  Kleinwort Benson v Malaysia Mining Corp Bhd (1989);
* a statement of opinion
  Bisset v Wilkinson (1927)
  Smith v Land & House Properties Ltd (1884);
* a statement of intention
  Edgington v Fitzmaurice (1885);
* a statement of law.

There must be an active representation – either in words or deed
'Silence does not amount to misrepresentation'.

Exceptions
* Facts selected to give a misleading impression:
  Dimmock v Hallett (1866).
* Where circumstances have changed:
  With v O'Flanagan (1936).
* Contracts *Uberrimae Fideii* – eg:
  contracts of insurance
  family arrangements
  fiduciary relationships.

It must have induced the relationship
* It must have been addressed to the party misled:
  Peek v Gurney (1893).

- It must have been a material inducement:
  Horsfall v Thomas (1862)
  Attwood v Small (1938).
- The fact that the representee did not take advantage of an opportunity to check is no defence:
  Redgrave v Hurd (1881).

Remedies for misrepresentation

Affirm the contract

Avoid the contract – using misrepresentation as a defence

Rescission – available for every kind of misrepresentation

Bars to rescission
- Affirmation of the contract:
  Long v Lloyd (1958).
- Lapse of time:
  Leaf v International Galleries (1950).
- Restitution must be possible:
  Erlanger v New Sombrero Phosphate Co Ltd (1878).
- A third party must not have acquired rights under the contract:
  Lewis v Avery (1973).

The court may order an indemnity to be paid in addition to rescission (*Whittington v Seale-Hayne* (1900)).

Damages
Damages are available in the following circumstances.

Damages for fraudulent misrepresentation in the tort of deceit
Derry v Peek (1889)

Damages for negligent misrepresentation
- In the tort of negligent statements under *Hedley Byrne v Heller & Partners* (1964).
- Under s 2(1) Misrepresentation Act 1967
  This is normally the most advantageous basis on which to sue for negligent misrepresentation as the plaintiff need only prove that the statements are untrue; it is up to the defendant to prove, if he can, that he had good grounds for making the statement (*Howard Marine & Dredging Co Ltd* (1978)).
  Damages are assessed on a reliance basis, as in tort.

The rules on remoteness of damage which apply to the tort of deceit apply, ie all losses directly flowing from the misrepresentation are covered, whether or not foreseeable:

Royscot Trust Ltd v Rogerson (1991)

Doyle v Olby Ltd (1969)

East v Maurer (1991)

Naughton v O'Callaghan (1990).

Damages for totally innocent misrepresentation

Damages may be awarded by court in lieu of rescission under s 2(2) Misrepresentation Act 1967.

If misrepresentation has become a term of the contract, damages for breach of contract are available.

Duress

Duress requires coercion, and renders a contract voidable. (see Rescission (above)).

Kind of duress

Duress to the person

Duress to goods

Economic duress – illegitimate commercial pressure

There must be two separate elements
- A coercion of the will ie the threatened party has no reasonable alternative open to him.
- An 'illegitimate' or unlawful threat, eg a threatened breach of contract:
  North Ocean Shipping Co Ltd v Hyundai Construction Co Ltd, The Atlantic Baron (1979)
  Universe Tankships Ltd of Monrovia v ITWF (1983)
  Pao On v Lau Yiu Long (1980)
  Atlas Express Ltd v Kafco (Importers and Distributors) (1989)
  Williams v Roffey Bros v Nicholls (Contractors) Ltd (1991)

Undue influence

Undue influence requires pressure which excludes a party from exercising free and independent judgment.

Undue influence renders a contract voidable (see rescission (above)).

Contracts where undue influence is presumed

The presumption arises from the relationship of the parties, either because:
- it falls within one of the five established relationships; or
- a relationship of trust has been built up over a period of time: *Lloyds Bank v Bundy* (1975).

The contract must be manifestly disadvantageous.

The stronger party may protect himself by insisting that the other party takes independent legal advice.

Contracts where undue influence must be proven

There must be evidence of some unfair or improper conduct.

The contract need not be manifestly disadvantageous: *CIBC Mortgages v Pitt* (1993).

A third party may be bound by the undue influence of a party to the contract

This may occur where:
- The party was acting as an agent of the third party: *Avon Finance v Bridger* (1985).
- The third party had actual or constructive knowledge of the possibility of undue influence:
  Barclays Bank v O'Brien (1993).
  Constructive notice occurs where the parties are in an emotional relationship, cohabiting, or where aged parents are involved; and one party is taking on a financial commitment which is not to his or her advantage and which advantages the other party.
  The third party may avoid undue influence by explaining fully his obligations to the party concerned, and advising him to take legal advice.

7 Illegality and capacity

ESSENTIALS

You should be familiar with the following areas:	✓
• the effect of illegality on a contract	
• the effect of a contract being void contrary to public policy	
• the identification of contracts in restraint of trade	
• the classification of minors contracts	
• the remedies available to the other party to a minors contract	
• the effect of contracts entered into by mentally disordered and drunken persons	

The main issue with regard to illegal contracts is the effect of illegality on a contract. The most often examined topic with regard to contracts which are declared void on grounds of public policy, are contracts in restraint of trade. These are the two topics which receive most attention here.

Illegal contracts

Contracts prohibited by statute

- Statute may declare a contract illegal, eg The Restrictive Trade Practices Act 1976.
- Statute may prohibit an act, but declare that it shall not effect validity of contract, eg The Trade Descriptions Act 1968.
- Statute may prohibit an act but may not stipulate its effect on the contract. The status of the contract will, in this case, be a matter of interpretation for the court.

In *Re Mahmoud & Isphani* (1921) the court decided that a statement that 'a person shall not buy or otherwise deal in linseed oil without a licence' was a prohibition, and a contract entered into by a person without a licence was therefore void.

The courts are reluctant to imply a prohibition when this is not clearly indicated in the statute.

Contracts illegal at common law

* An agreement to commit a crime, a tort or a fraud, eg to defraud the rating authority (*Allen v Roscous* (1676)); to publish a libel (*Clay v Yates* (1865)).
* An agreement to defraud the revenue (*Napier v Business Associates* (1951)).
* Contracts damaging to the country's safety or foreign relations.
* Contracts interfering with the course of justice, eg contracts to give false evidence.
* Contracts leading to corruption in public life (*Parkinson v Royal College of Ambulance* (1925)).
* Contracts tending to promote sexual immorality (*Pearce v Brooks* (1866)).

Effects of illegality

There are conflicting policies influencing the law with regard to the effect of illegality on a contract.

On the one hand:
* It is necessary to discourage the formation of an illegal contract.
* The law should not be seen to be enforcing illegal contracts.

On the other hand:
* Not all illegal contracts are equally reprehensible.
* Both parties may not be equally at fault.
* There is a need to prevent unjust enrichment.
* Deterrence is a matter for the criminal not the civil law.
* The principle of freedom of contract.
A contract may be affected by illegality in two ways.

Contracts illegal as formed, ie a contract illegal in its inception

Such contracts are void *ab initio*

There can be no action for breach of contract. In *Pearce v Brooks* (1866) the owner of a coach of unusual design, was unable to recover the cost of hire from a prostitute who, to his knowledge, had hired it in order to attract clients (unjust enrichment).

Money paid, or property transferred under the contract cannot be recovered

In *Parkinson v Royal College of Ambulance* (1925) Parkinson was unable to recover the money he had donated to the defendants on the understanding that they would obtain a knighthood for him.

Exceptions

- Where the parties are not *in pari delicto*, eg where one party is unaware of the illegal nature of the contract, or has been induced to enter into it by fraudulent misrepresentation, or is the party the law was attempting to protect, eg a tenant who had paid an illegal premium could recover it (*Kiriri Cotton Co v Dewani* (1960)).
- Where the transferor genuinely repents, and repudiates the contract before performance. In *Bigos v Boustead* (1951) however, the court was not convinced that the plaintiff had genuinely repented.
- Where the transferor can frame his claim without relying on the contract. In *Bowmakers Ltd v Barnet Instruments Ltd* (1945) the plaintiffs delivered machine tools to the defendants under illegal hire-purchase contracts contrary to the Defence Regulations. It was held they could succeed in a claim for possession in the tort of conversion. Similarly, in *Tinsley v Milligan* (1993) both parties had contributed money towards the purchase of a house, but the house had been put in the name of Tinsley alone in order to allow Milligan to make various social security claims. When Milligan sued for the return of the money, it was argued that the agreement had been entered into for an illegal purpose, and that the public conscience 'would be affronted by recognising rights created by illegal transactions'. The House of Lords held, however, that a resulting trust had been created in favour of Milligan by the contribution to the purchase price. Milligan, therefore, could rely on the resulting trust and had no need to rely on the illegal agreement. This case shows (a) that the rule applies to equity as well as to common law; (b) the test of 'affront to the public conscience' developed by the Court of Appeal and applied to this case by the Court of Appeal, is not good law.

Collateral contracts are tainted with the illegality and are void

For example, a promissory note issued in connection with the contract.

Where part of the contract is lawful, the court will not sever the good from the bad

In *Napier v National Business Agency* (1951) certain payments were described as 'expenses' in order to defraud the Inland Revenue. The court refused to enforce payment of the accompanying salary, as the whole contract was tainted with the illegality.

Contracts illegal in their performance

For instance, the illegality may only arise during the performance of a contract, eg a carrier may break the law by exceeding the speed limit whilst delivering goods belonging to a client. He will be punished, but the contract will not necessarily be void.

* A claim by the innocent party to enforce the contract in these cases is strong

  In *Marles v Philip Trant* (1954) X sold the defendant winter wheat described as spring wheat, which the defendant then resold to the plaintiff, again describing it as spring wheat. The defendant did not deliver an invoice along with seeds as required by statute. It was held that the plaintiff could sue for damages for breach of contract. The contract was illegal in its performance, but not in its inception.

  In *Strongman v Simcock* (1955) Simcock failed to get licences which were needed to modernise some houses which belonged to him, and refused to pay for the work on the basis that the contracts were illegal. It was held that Strongman could not sue on the illegal contracts, but could sue Simcock on his collateral promise to obtain the licences.

  In *Archbold v Spanglett* (1951) Spanglett contracted to carry Archbold's whisky in a van which was not licensed to carry any goods other than his own. Archbold was unaware of this and could, therefore, recover damages for breach of contract.

  But, in *Ashmore, Benson, Pease & Co v AV Dawson Ltd* (1973), the other party knew of the overloading of the lorry, and could not therefore recover damages. He had participated in the illegality.

* Even the guilty party may enforce the contract, if the illegality is incidental

  In *Shaw v Groom* (1970) a landlord failed to give his tenant a rent book as required by law. It was held that he could sue for the rent. The purpose of the statute was to punish the landlord's failure to provide a rent book not to render the contract void.

  In *St John's Shipping v Rank* (1957) a shipowner overloaded his ship in contravention of a statute. It was held that he was still able to recover freight. The purpose of the statute was to penalise overloading, not to make the contract illegal.

However, in *Anderson v Daniel* (1924) a seller was prohibited from suing for the price of fertiliser he had delivered without an invoice as this was contrary to law.

Contracts void at common law on grounds of public policy

Contracts damaging to the institution of marriage

For example, contracts in restraint of marriage; marriage brokerage contracts; contracts for future separation (pre-nuptial agreements). Contracts made after or immediately before separation are valid.

Contracts to oust the jurisdiction of the courts

Arbitration clauses, however, are valid.

Contracts in restraint of trade

A contract in restraint of trade is *prima facie* void, but the courts will now uphold the restriction if it is shown that:

- the restraint is reasonable between the parties;
- the restraint is reasonable as regards the interest of the public.

In *Esso Petroleum v Harpers Garage (Stourport) Ltd* (1968) it was stated that the court will consider:

- Whether the contract is in restraint of trade
  A contract is in restraint of trade if it restricts a person's liberty to carry on his trade or profession. Certain restraints, however, have become acceptable over the years, eg 'tied houses', restrictive covenants in leases; sole agency, or sole distributorship agreements.
- Whether it should nevertheless be enforced because it is reasonable
  The onus of proving reasonability is on the promisee. The court must scrutinise the restraint in the light of the circumstances existing at the time the contract was made. A restraint to be permissible must be no wider than is necessary to protect the relevant interest of the promisee.
  The court will first consider reasonability from the point of view of the parties. It will then consider the public interest. It has been sug-

gested that employment or sale of business agreements are unlikely to be declared invalid on the grounds of the public interest if they are reasonable as far as the parties themselves are concerned, but a 'solus' agreement, or an agreement between companies not to compete (now controlled by statute) are more likely to harm the interests of the public.

Categories of contracts in restraint of trade

Restraints on employees
The restraint is void, unless the employer can show:
- It is necessary to protect a proprietory interest, ie *trade secrets* or *trade connections*. A restraint merely to prevent competition will not be enforced.

In *Foster v Suggett* (1918) a works manager was instructed in certain confidential methods of glass-making. The contract forbade him from being interested in any other glass-making concerns within the UK for five years. It was held that the restriction was valid.

In *Fitch v Dewes* (1921) a solicitor's clerk was forbidden to work within five miles of Tamworth Town Hall. It was held that the solicitor had trade connections to protect and the restraint was valid.

In *Eastham v Newcastle United Football Club* (1964) the court accepted that the proper organisation of football was a valid matter for clubs to protect, but found the 'retain and transfer system' unreasonable.

- The restraint is no greater than is necessary to protect the employer's interest in terms of time and area.

In *Scorer v Seymore-Johns* (1966) the court upheld a restriction of 10 miles within branch A at which the employee had worked, but held that a similar restraint covering branch B at which the employee had not worked was unreasonable and void.

Problems with area can be overcome by using 'non-solicitation' clauses instead.

In *Home Counties Dairies v Skilton* (1970) a milk roundsman agreed that for one year after leaving his present job, he would not sell milk to his employers' customers. It was held that the restraint was valid; it was necessary to protect the employer against loss of customers.

The validity of the duration of the restraint depends on the nature of the business to be protected, and on the status of the employee.

In *Briggs v Oates* (1991) a restriction of five miles for five years on an assistant solicitor was upheld as reasonable.

A restraint imposed by indirect means, eg by loss of pension rights (*Bull v Pitney-Bowes Ltd* (1967)) or where two companies agreed not to take on each others employees (*Kores v Kolok* (1959)) will be judged by the same criteria.

Restraints on the vendor of a business

Such a restraint is valid if it is intended to protect the purchaser's interest in the goodwill of the business bought.

In *Vancouver Malt & Sake Brewing Co v Vancouver Breweries Ltd* (1934) a company which was licensed to brew beer, but which had not at any time brewed beer, was sold. The buyer agreed not to brew any beer for 15 years. It was held that the restraint was void. Since there was no goodwill of a beer brewing business to be transferred, the restraint was merely a restriction on competition.

In *British Concrete v Schelff* (1921) S sold his localised business to B who had branches all over the UK and agreed not to open any business within 10 miles of any of B's branches. It was held that the restriction was void; B was entitled only to protect the business he had bought, not the business which he already owned.

In *Nordenfeldt v Maxim Nordenfeldt Co Ltd* (1894) N, a word-wide supplier of guns, sold his world-wide business to M, and agreed not to manufacture guns anywhere in the world for 25 years. It was held that the restriction was valid.

Exclusive dealing agreements

- 'Solus' agreements (whereby A agrees to buy all his requirements of a particular commodity from B)

  In *Esso Petroleum v Harpers Garage Ltd* (1968) a solus agreement for four years was held reasonable, but a solus agreement for 21 years was held unreasonable, and therefore void.

  Solus agreements were distinguished from restrictive covenants in a lease. When an oil company leases a filling station to X, inserting a clause that X should buy all it requirements from the company, this is not subject to restraint of trade rules because the tenant is not giving up a previously held freedom.

  But in *Amoco v Rocca Bros* (1975) Rocca leased a filling station to Amoco who immediately leased it back to him. It was held that restraint of trade rules did apply.

  In *Alec Lobb (Garages) v Total Oil Ltd* (1985) in a similar lease-back arrangement, a solus agreement for between seven and 21 years was held reasonable on the ground that the arrangement was a rescue operation benefitting the plaintiffs. The fact that there were 'break' clauses in the underlease was also relevant.

- Exclusive services contracts

  Most exclusive services contracts are found in professional sport or entertainment.

In *Schroeder Music Publishing Co v Macaulay* (1974) it was held that a contract, by which an unknown song writer undertook to give his exclusive services to a publisher who made no promise to publish his work, was subject to the restraint of trade doctrine, as it was 'capable of enforcement in an oppressive manner'.

In *Greig v Insole* (1978) the MCC banned any cricketer who played for a cricketing 'circus' from playing for England. The court held that the ban was void as being in restraint of trade.

It has been suggested that the courts will hold exclusive dealing and service contracts to be within the restraint of trade doctrine, if they contain unusual or novel features, or if there is disparity in the bargaining power, and the agreement is likely to cause hardship to the weaker party.

Cartel agreements

These are now covered by statute, eg The Fair Trading Act 1973, The Resale Prices Act 1976, The Restrictive Trade Practices Act 1976, The Competition Act 1980, and The Treaty of Rome.

Effect of restraint

Unless reasonable, the restraint is void. A void restraint is severable. Severance can be operated in two ways:

- Severance of the whole of the objectionable promise. If this is done, the rest of the contract is valid and enforceable. Severance of a whole promise is not possible, however, where it is the whole of the consideration supplied by one party.
- Severance of the objectionable part of the promise.

Two tests must be satisfied:

- The 'blue pencil' test
  It must be possible to sever the illegal part simply by deleting words in the contract. The court will not add words, substitute one word for another, or rearrange words or in any way redraft the contract. In *Mason v Provident Clothing & Supply Co Ltd* (1913), the House of Lords refused to redraft a promise not to work within 25 miles of London, but in *Goldsoll v Goldman* (1915) a dealer in imitation jewellery promised not to deal in real or imitation jewellery either in the UK or abroad. Dealing in real jewellery and dealing abroad was severed.
- Severance of the objectionable part of the contract must not alter the nature (as distinct from the extent) of the original contract

The illegal restraint will not be severed if it is the the main purpose of the restraint, or if to sever it would alter entirely the scope and intention of the agreement. In *Attwood v Lamont* (1920) the court refused to sever restrictions on a tailor from competing with any department of the department store which had employed him. The court stated that this was a covenant 'which must stand or fall in its unaltered form'.

Capacity

Only the capacity of minors, persons of unsound mind and drunken persons will be dealt with here.

Minors

A minor is a person under the age of 18 according to the Family Law Reform Act 1969.

The law pursues two conflicting policies in the case of minors. On the one hand, it tries to protect minors from their own inexperience and, on the other, it tries to ensure that persons dealing with minors are not dealt with in a harsh manner.

Contracts with minors can be divided into three categories.

Valid contracts – contracts which can be enforced against a minor

Contracts for necessaries
Necessary goods are defined in The Sale of Goods Act 1979 as 'goods suitable to his condition in life, and to his actual requirements at the time of sale and delivery'.

In *Nash v Inman* (1908) a student purchased 11 silk waistcoats while still a minor. The court held that silk waistcoats were suitable to the conditions of life of a Cambridge undergraduate at that time, but they were not suitable to his actual needs since he already had a sufficient supply of waistcoats.

It is important to distinguish between luxurious goods of utility, and goods of pure luxury. The status of the minor can make the former into necessaries, but the latter can never be classified as necessaries.

The burden of proving that the goods are necessaries are on the seller.

Necessary services include education, medical and legal services and they must satisfy the same tests as necessary goods.

Professor Treitel considers that both executed and unexecuted contracts for necessaries can be enforced. He cites *Robert v Gray* (1919) where Roberts agreed to take Gray, a minor, on a billiard tour to instruct him in the profession of billiard player. Gray repudiated the contract. The court held that Roberts could recover damages despite the fact that the contract was executory.

Cheshire, Fifoot and Furmston agree that executory contracts for necessary services are enforceable as in *Roberts v Gray* but deny that executory contracts for necessary goods can be enforced. They cite:

- the actual wording of the Sale of Goods Act which refers to time of 'sale and delivery';
- the minor has to pay a reasonable price for the goods not the contractual price.

These indicate, it is argued, that liability is based on acceptance of the goods, not on agreement.

Beneficial contracts of service

These must be for the benefit of the minor.

In *De Fransesco v Barnum* (1890) the terms of the contract were burdensome and harsh on the minor. The court held that the contract was therefore void.

However, in *Doyle v White City Stadium* (1935) a minor had forfeited his payment for a fight because the contract provided that this should happen if a boxer was disqualified for fouling. It was held that the contract, which was provided by the Boxing Board of Control, was enforceable against the minor. Where a contract is, on the whole, for the benefit of a minor, it will not be invalidated because one term has operated in a way which is not to his advantage.

Beneficial contracts must be contracts of service or similar to a contract of service. In *Chaplin v Leslie Frewin (Publishers) Ltd* (1966) the court enforced a contract by a minor to publish his memoirs since this would train him in becoming an author, and enable him to earn a living. But trading contracts (involving the minor's capital) will not be enforced even if it does help the minor earn a living. In *Mercantile Union Guarantee Co Ltd v Ball* (1937) the court refused to enforce a hire purchase contract for a lorry which would enable a minor to trade as a haulage contractor.

Voidable contracts

Voidable contracts can be avoided by the minor before majority or within a short time afterwards. They comprise contracts of continuing obligation such as contracts to acquire an interest in land, or partly paid shares, or partnership agreements.

The minor can free himself from obligations under these contracts for the future, eg an obligation to pay rent under a lease, but will have to pay for benefits already received. He cannot recover money already paid under the contract unless there has been a total failure of consideration (*Steinberg v Scala (Leeds) Ltd* (1923)).

Other contracts

Other contracts cannot be enforced against a minor.

But

- The minor himself may enforce such contracts.
- Property can pass under such contracts.
- Where the contract has been carried out by the minor, he cannot recover any property unless there has been a total failure of consideration, or some other failing which would equally apply to an adult.
- The Minors Contracts Act 1987 provides that:
  (a) a minor may ratify such a contract on majority, and it can thereafter be enforced against him;
  (b) a guarantee of a minor's debt will not be void because a minor's debt is unenforceable against him;
  (c) a court may, if it considers it just and equitable to do so, order a minor to return property he has received under a void contract or any property representing it. It is not clear whether property transferred under the contract covers money eg in money lending contracts. It is argued that as 'property representing it' must cover money, it would, therefore, be illogical to exclude money acquired directly, but there is as yet no decision on this point. Property cannot presumably be recovered under this section where the minor has given away the contract property.
- Equity will order restitution of property acquired by fraud, but there can be no restitution of money (*Leslie v Sheill* (1914)) and no restitution if the minor has resold the property.
- An action may be brought in tort if it does not in any way rely on the contract. But although a minor is fully liable for all his torts, he may not be sued in tort if this is just an indirect way of enforcing a contract. In *Leslie v Sheill* (1914) a minor obtained a loan by fraudulently misrepresenting his age. It was held that he could not be sued in the tort of deceit since this would be an indirect way of enforcing a contract which was void.

Persons of unsound mind and drunken persons

A person who has been declared a 'patient' under The Mental Health Act 1983 by the Court of Protection is incapable of entering into a valid contract.

Other mentally disordered persons and drunken persons will be bound by their contracts unless:

• they were so disordered or drunk that they did not understand the nature of what they were doing; and
• the other party was aware of this.

Such contracts may be affirmed during a sober or lucid moment.

The Sale of Goods Act requires that where 'necessaries are sold and delivered to a person who by reason of mental incapacity or drunkenness is incompetent to contract, he must pay a reasonable price for them'.

Revision Notes

Illegal contracts

Contracts prohibited by statute

Where a statute makes the commission of an act an offence, the courts must interpret that statute to discover whether a contract involving that act is also rendered void, or whether the penalty provided by the statute is thought a sufficient sanction and the contract may be enforced.

Contracts illegal at common law on grounds of public policy

These include agreements to commit a crime, a fraud, a tort; to damage the country's foreign relations or safety; to interfere with the course of justice; to promote corruption or sexual immorality.

Effects of illegality

The effect of illegality depends on whether the purpose of the contract was illegal (illegal as formed) or whether the purpose was legal but there was some illegality in the way the contract was carried out (illegal as performed).

Contracts illegal as formed
The contract is void: no action for breach of contract:
Pearce v Brooks (1866).

Money paid or property transferred cannot be recovered.

Exceptions
- Where the parties are not *in pari delicto*.
- Where the transferor genuinely repents:
  Bigos v Boustead (1951).
- Where the transferor can frame his claim in tort (without relying on contract).

Collateral contracts are tainted with illegality and are void.

Where part of the contract is lawful, the court will not sever the good from the bad:
Napier v National Business Agency (1951).

Contracts illegal in their performance

The innocent party may enforce the contract:
Marles v Philip Trant (1954)
Strongman v Sincock (1955)
Archbold v Spanglett (1951).

The guilty party may also enforce the contract if the illegality is incidental:
Shaw v Groom (1970)
St John Shipping v Rank (1957)
cf *Anderson v Daniel* (1924).

Contracts declared void at common law on grounds of public policy

Effect of the contract being void

* The contract is void – there can be no action for breach of contract.
* Money paid or property transferred under the contract can be recovered.
* Collateral contracts will be enforced.
* The court may be prepared to sever the good from the bad.

Contracts in restraint of trade

Contracts in restraint of trade are those which restrict a person's freedom to carry on his trade or profession. They are valid only if reasonable as between the parties, and from the point of view of the public.

Restraints on employees

These are valid only if there is a valid proprietory interest to protect, eg trade secrets or trade connections; and the restraint is no wider in terms of time and area than is necessary to protect that proprietory interest:
Foster v Suggett (1918)
Fitch v Dewes (1921)
Home Counties Dairies v Skilton (1970).

Restraints on the vendor of a business

The restraint is reasonable if it protects only the business that has changed hands. The vendor is not entitled to protect any other business he may own:
British Concrete v Schelff (1921)
Nordenfeldt v Maxim Nordenfeldt Co Ltd (1894).

Exclusive dealing and exclusive services agreements

The courts will hold these agreements unreasonable only if they contain unusual or novel features, or there is an unbalance in the bargaining power of the parties, or the agreement is likely to cause hardship to the weaker party:
Esso Petroleum v Harpers Garage Ltd (1968)
Schroeder Music Publishing Co v Macaulay (1974).

Severability of void restraints

The court may sever:
- the whole of a void restraint, leaving an enforceable contract.
- the objectionable part of the restraint only, provided the severance satisfies the 'blue pencil test', and does not alter the nature of the restraint.

Capacity

Minors, ie persons under 18.
Minors' contracts fall into three categories.

Valid contracts – contracts which can be enforced against a minor

- Contracts for 'necessary goods and services'.
  These must be appropriate to his status and actual requirements:
  Nash v Inman (1908).
  There is a dispute as to whether such unexecuted contracts can be enforced:
  Roberts v Gray (1919).
- Beneficial contracts of service
  The contract as a whole must be examined to see whether it is beneficial to the minor:

De Fransesco v Barnum (1890)
Doyle v White City Stadium (1935).
They must be both beneficial and a contract of service or similar:
Chaplin v Leslie Frewin (Publishers) Ltd (1966).
A trading contract will not be enforced, however beneficial:
Mercantile Union Guarantee Co v Ball (1937).

Contracts voidable by the minor before majority or within a short time afterwards

For example, leases.

They can be avoided for the future but benefits already gained must be paid for:
Steinberg v Scala (Leeds) Ltd (1923).

Contracts which are void

That is, all other contracts. But such contracts are not without legal effect, eg
* property can pass;
* the minor cannot recover property passed under an executed contract unless there has been a total failure of consideration;
* the minor himself can enforce the contract and can ratify it at the age of majority;
* the other party may not enforce the contract, but can recover property he has transferred at the discretion of the court (Minors Contracts Act 1987) or, if there has been fraud (in equity):
Leslie v Sheill (1914).

8 Discharge

You should be familiar with the following areas:

- discharge by performance
- discharge by agreement
- discharge as a result of a breach
- discharge by frustration
- the effect of frustration

A contract is discharged when there are no obligations outstanding under that contract.

It may be discharged by performance, by agreement, as the result of a breach, or by frustration.

Performance

Precision of performance

To discharge obligations under a contract, a party must perform exactly what was promised. In *Cutter v Powell* (1795) a ship's engineer undertook to sail a ship from Jamaica to Liverpool, but died before the voyage was complete. It was held that nothing could be recovered in respect of his service; he had not fulfilled his obligation.

In *Bolton v Mahadeva* (1972) the contract was for the installation of a central heating system. The system as installed gave out less heat than it should, and there were fumes in one room. It was held that the contractor could not claim payment; although the boiler and pipes had been installed, they did not fulfil the primary purpose of heating the house. These are examples of 'entire' contracts which consist of one unseverable obligation. See also *Sumpter v Hedges* (1898).

Despite the rule that performance must be exact, the law will allow payment to be made, on a *quantum meruit* basis, for incomplete performance in the following circumstances:

- Where the contract is divisible, payment can be recovered for the completed part, eg goods delivered by instalments.
- Where the promisee has freedom of choice and accepts partial performance. In *Sumpter v Hedges* (1898), however, payment for partial performance was refused as Hedges had been left with a half-built house, and had been put in a position where he had no choice but to accept partial performance.
- Where the promisee prevents complete performance; eg in *Planche v Colbourn* (1831) a writer was allowed payment for the work he had already done when the publisher abandoned the series.
- Where the promisor has performed a substantial part of the contract. In *Hoenig v Isaacs* (1952) the plaintiff decorated the defendant's flat, but because of faulty workmanship the defendant had to pay £55 to another firm to finish the job. It was held that the plaintiff was entitled to £750 (the contract price) minus the £55 paid to the other firm (cf *Bolton v Mahadeva* (1972) where the court declined to find substantial performance).

This has become known as the doctrine of substantial performance. In order to rely on this doctrine the plaintiff's failure to perform must amount only to a breach of warranty or a non-fundamental breach of an innominate term. It will not apply to a fundamental breach or to a breach of condition.

It has also been suggested that it applies to faulty performance rather than incomplete performance.

Time of performance

Equity considers that time is not 'of the essence of a contract' ie a condition, except in the following circumstances:

- It is stipulated in the contract (see *Lombard North Central v Butterworth* (Chapter 4)).
- One party has given notice during the currency of the contract that performance must take place within a certain time.
  Reasonable notice must be given. In *Rickards v Oppenheim* (1950) a car body which had been ordered from the plaintiffs was late. The defendants gave final notice to the plaintiff that unless it was delivered within three months they would cancel the order. It was held that time had been made of the essence; the defendants could cancel the order.
- The nature of the contract makes it imperative that stipulations as to time should be observed, eg contracts for the sale of perishable goods.

The LPA 1925 stipulated that terms as to the time of performance should be interpreted in the same way at common law as in equity. In *Raineri v Miles* (1981) the House of Lords held that that meant that late performance would not give rise to a right to terminate, but would give rise to damages.

Tender of performance

If one party tenders performance which is refused, he or she may sue for breach of contract.

If payment is tendered and rejected, the obligation to tender payment is discharged but the obligation to pay remains.

Agreement

As contracts are created by agreement, so they may be discharged by agreement. Consideration is necessary to make the agreement binding. Discharge by agreement may be:

* In accordance with a term in the original contract
  (a) a 'condition subsequent' – the contract ends automatically on the happening of a future event; or
  (b) a term describing the way in which the contract may be terminate, eg by notice.

* In accordance with a new agreement
  Consideration is needed to make the new agreement binding.
  (a) a bilateral discharge, ie the contract is wholly executory – there is no problem with consideration since both parties surrender their rights under the contract.
  (b) a unilateral discharge, ie the contract is partly executed – one party has completed their performance under the contract. To make the agreement binding there must either be a deed (a 'release') or new consideration ('accord and satisfaction') or the doctrine of equitable estoppel or waiver must apply (see Chapter 2).

Breach

A breach does not of itself discharge a contract. It may allow the other party an option to treat the contract as discharged, ie to terminate the contract, if the breach is sufficiently serious, ie if it is:

- a breach of condition (see Chapter 3);
- a fundamental breach of an innominate term (see Chapter 3);
- a repudiation.

There are special problems where a party repudiates a contract under a wrong assumption that he has a right to do so.

In *Federal Commerce & Navigation v Molena Alpha* (1979) the owners of a ship gave instructions not to issue bills of lading without which the charterers could not operate the ship. They wrongly believed that they had the right to do so. It was held that their conduct constituted a wrongful repudiation of the contract which allowed the other party to treat the contract as discharged.

In *Woodar Investment Development Ltd v Wimpey Construction Ltd* (1980) the purchaser repudiated a contract for the sale of land, wrongly believing that he had a right to do so. It was held not to be a wrongful repudiation which allowed the other party to treat the contract as discharged.

Cheshire, Fifoot and Furmston have distinguished the two decisions on the basis that there was no urgency in *Woodar* since the time for completion was some way off and the seller could have sued for breach of contract. In *Alpha Modena*, on the other hand, the time before performance was very short, putting much greater pressure on the charterers.

Effect of treating the contract as discharged

The obligation of both parties to perform (ie the primary obligation) is discharged from the date of the termination. However, a secondary obligation to pay damages for any losses caused to the innocent party as a result of the breach then comes into operation. The innocent party may recover damages to cover both past and future losses (*Lombard North Central v Butterworth* (1987)).

Although the contract is terminated, it will be taken into consideration in assessing any future losses. In *The Mihalis Angelos* (1971) a ship was due in Haiphong on about 1 July. If it was not there by 20 July, the contract could be cancelled. On 17 July it was obvious the ship could not reach Haiphong by 20 July. The charterers cancelled. It was held to be wrongful repudiation. The charterers had no right to cancel until 20 July. However, only nominal damages were awarded. The court could consult the contract in order to assess damages. The fact that the ship could not have reached Haiphong by 20 July was relevant.

The discharge does not operate retrospectively. In *Photo Production v Securicor* (1986) Securicor was able to rely on an exclusion clause in the contract to cover its fundamental breach.

The decision to terminate cannot be retracted.

Anticipatory breach of contract

A party may announce, in advance, that it does not intend to carry out the terms of a contract. This is an anticipatory breach of contract, and may be either:

- explicit, as in *Hochster v De La Tour* (1853) where a travel courier announced in advance that he would not be fulfiling his contract;
- implicit as in *Frost v Knight* (1972) where a party disabled himself from carrying out a promise to marry by marrying another person.

Effect of an anticipatory breach of contract

The other party may sue for damages immediately. He or she does not have to await the date of performance (*Hochster v De La Tour* 1853)).

The innocent party may refuse to accept the repudiation. They may affirm the contract and continue to perform their obligations under the contract.

In *White & Carter Ltd v McGregor* (1962), the defendants cancelled a contract shortly after it had been signed. The plaintiffs refused to accept the cancellation and carried on with the contract. They then sued for the full contract price. It was held that the plaintiffs were entitled to succeed; a repudiation does not automatically bring a contract to an end; the innocent party has an option either to affirm the contract or to terminate the contract. The rule however, is subject to two limitations:

- The innocent party must be able to fulfil the contract without the cooperation of the other party. In *Hounslow UDC v Twickenham Garden Developments Ltd* (1971) Hounslow council cancelled a contract to lay out a park. It was held that the defendants could not rely on *White and Carter v McGregor* because a considerable amount of co-operation from the council was required, and the work was to be performed on council property.
- The innocent party must have had a legitimate interest, financial or otherwise, in performing the contract, rather than in claiming damages. In *The Alaskan Trader* (1984) a ship chartered to the defendants required extensive repairs at the end of the first year, whereupon the defendants repudiated the contract. The plaintiffs, however,

refused to accept the repudiation, repaired the ship, and kept it fully crewed ready for the defendant's use. It was held that the plaintiffs had no special interest in keeping the contract alive. They should have accepted the repudiation and sued for damages.

Where a party has affirmed the contract

- The party will have to pay damages for any subsequent breach; he cannot argue that the other party's anticipatory breach excuses him (*Fercometal SARL v Mediterranean Shipping Co* (1988)).
- There is a danger that a supervening event may frustrate the contract and deprive the innocent party of his right to damages, as in *Avery v Bowden* (1855) (below).

Frustration

Definition of frustration

Frustration occurs where it is established that, due to a subsequent change in circumstances, the contract has become impossible to perform, or it has been deprived of its commercial purpose.

The doctrine has been kept to narrow limits by the courts who have insisted that the supervening event must destroy a fundamental assumption, and by business men who have 'drafted out' the doctrine by *force majeure* clauses.

The basis of the doctrine and the tests

Until the 19th century, the courts adhered to a theory of 'absolute contracts', as in *Paradine v Jane* (1647). It was said that if the parties wished to evade liability because of some supervening event, then they should provide for this in the contract. However, in *Taylor v Caldwell* (1863) the courts relented, and held that if the contract became impossible to perform due to some extraneous cause for which neither party was responsible, then the contact would be discharged. The doctrine was originally based on the presumed intention of the parties.

In *Taylor v Caldwell* (1863) the court stated 'the contract is subject to an implied term that the parties should be excused if, before the breach, performance becomes impossible'. The 'implied term' test contributed greatly to the development of the doctrine of consideration, but it has been criticised since it involved the court in implying a term to cover what the parties had not contemplated.

The doctrine would now seem to be based on the court imposing a just solution. Lord Wright has stated that the 'court ... decides the question in accordance with what seems just and reasonable'. Lord Simon in *National Carriers v Panalpina Ltd* (1981) stated 'supervenes an event which significantly changes the nature of the outstanding contractual rights ... that it would be unjust to hold the parties to them'.

The 'implied term' test would now seem to be replaced by the 'radical change in obligation' test which is applied in order to decide what is 'just and equitable'.

In *Davies Contractors v Fareham UDC* (1956), Lord Radcliff stated that: 'Frustration occurs where to require performance would be to require something radically different from what was undertaken.'

It has been suggested that a three-tier test should be applied. The contractual terms should be construed in the light of the circumstances at the time the contract was created. The new circumstances should be examined to decide what would happen if the existing terms were applied. The two contractual obligations should be compared to see if there is a radical or fundamental change.

Note

It is not the circumstances but the nature of the obligation which must have changed.

It is not hardship or inconvenience or material loss alone which calls the principles of frustration into play. There must be, as well, such a change in the significance of the obligation that the thing undertaken would, if performed, be a different thing from that contracted for.

Circumstances in which frustration may occur

The subject matter of the contract has been destroyed, or is otherwise unavailable

In *Taylor v Caldwell* (1863) a contract to hire a music hall was held to be frustrated by the destruction of the music hall by fire (see also s 7 Sale of Goods Act 1979).

But the unavailable or destroyed object must have been intended by both parties to be the subject of the contract.

In *Blackburn Bobbin & Co v Allen* (1918) the contract was for the sale of 'birch timber' which the seller intended to obtain from Finland. It was held that the contract was not frustrated when it became impossible to obtain timber from Finland. The subject matter of the contract was birch timber not Finnish birch timber.

Death or incapacity of a party to a contract of personal service, or a contract where the personality of one party is important

In *Condor v The Barron Knights* (1966) a contract between a pop group and its drummer was held frustrated when the drummer became ill and was unable to fulfil the terms of the contract. A claim for unfair dismissal can also sometimes be defeated by the defence of frustration where an employee has become permanently incapacitated or imprisoned for a long period.

The contract has become illegal to perform

This may be either because of a change in the law, or the outbreak of war. In *Avery v Bowden* (1855) a contract to supply goods to Russia was frustrated when the Crimean War broke out on the ground that it had become an illegal contract – trading with the enemy.

Note

The outbreak of war between two foreign states, however, will not render a contract illegal, but may make it impossible to perform. In *Finelvet v Vinava Shipping Co Ltd* (1983) a contract to deliver goods to Basra, did not become illegal on the outbreak of the Iraq-Iran war, but was frustrated when it became too dangerous to sail to Basra.

Establishing whether a contract is impossible or illegal to perform is relatively straightforward, but it is more difficult to decide whether the commercial purpose of the contract has failed. It may happen in the following circumstances.

Failure of an event upon which the contract was based

In *Krell v Henry* (1903), the court held that a contract to hire a room overlooking the proposed route of the coronation procession was frustrated when the coronation was postponed. The purpose of the contract was to view the coronation, not merely to hire a room. It has been argued that the fact that the hire of the room was a 'one-off' transaction was important. The judge in the case contrasted it with the hire of a taxi to take to client to Epsom on Derby day. This would be a normal contractual transaction for the taxi driver, the cancellation of the Derby would not, therefore, frustrate the contract. In the case of *Herne Bay v Hutton* (1903) the court refused to hold frustrated a contract to hire a boat to see the King review the fleet when the review was cancelled; the fleet was still there and could be viewed – there was, therefore, no complete failure of the purpose of the contract.

Government interference or delay

In *Metropolitan Water Board v Dick Kerr & Co* (1918) a contract had been formed in 1913 to build a reservoir within six years. In 1915, the government ordered the work to be stopped and the plant sold. It was held that the the contract was frustrated.

In *Jackson v Union Marine* (1874) a ship was chartered in November to proceed with all dispatch to Newport. It did not reach Newport until the following August. It was held that the contract was frustrated since the ship was not available for the voyage for which she had been chartered.

In *The Nema* (1982) it was stated that whether the delay would frustrate a contract would depend on whether it would make performance radically different from that contemplated in the contract. In that case a charter party was frustrated when a long strike closed the port at which the ship was due to load, so that of the six or seven voyages contracted to be made between April and December, only two could be made.

Similar difficulties arise in the case of contracts of employment (illness or imprisonment) and leases. It has been suggested that where the contract is of a fixed duration, and the unavailability of the subject matter is only temporary, the court should consider the ratio of the likely interruption to the duration of the contract.

Leases

It had long been thought that the doctrine of frustration did not apply to leases (see *Paradine v Jane and Cricklewood Investments v Leightons Investments* (1945)).

However, in *National Carriers v Panalpina* (1981) the House of Lords declared that, in principle, a lease could be frustrated. In that case, a street which gave the only access to a warehouse was closed for 18 months. The lease for the warehouse was for 10 years. It was held that the lease was not frustrated.

The House of Lords did state, however, that where there was only one purpose for the land/property leased, and this purpose became impossible, then the lease would be frustrated, eg a short term holiday lease.

Limits to the doctrine of frustration

Doctrine must be kept within narrow limits.

It will not be applied:
- On the grounds of inconvenience, increase in expense, loss of profit

In *Davies Contractors Ltd v Fareham UDC* (1956) the contractors had agreed to build a council estate at a fixed price. Due to strikes, bad weather, shortages of labour and materials, there were considerable delays and the houses could only be built at a substantial loss. It was held that the contract was not frustrated; 'hardship or inconvenience, or material loss' do not themselves frustrate a contract. See also the *Suez* cases where the courts refused to hold shipping contracts, frustrated as a result of the closing of the Suez Canal, unless the contracts specified a route through the canal. In other cases, the contracts were merely inconvenient or expensive to perform.

- Where there is an express provision in the contract covering the intervening event (ie a *force majeure* clause)

But a *force majeure* clause will be interpreted narrowly as in *Metropolitan Water Board v Dick Kerr & Co* (1918) where a reference to 'delays' was held to refer only to ordinary delays, and not to a delay caused by government decree.

A *force majeure* clause will not in any case be applied to cover trading with an enemy.

- Where the frustration is self-induced

A contract will not be frustrated if the event making performance impossible was the voluntary action of one of the parties. If the party concerned had a choice open to him, and chose to act in such a way as to make performance impossible, then the frustration will be self-induced and the court will refuse to treat the contract as discharged.

In *Maritime National Fish v Ocean Trawlers* (1935) the plaintiffs chartered a trawler from the defendants which both knew could only be operated under a government licence. The plaintiffs were awarded only three licences, instead of the five they sought. They allocated these to their own trawlers, and returned the hired trawler to the defendants. The court held that the contract was not frustrated since the failure to use the vessel was self-induced.

The rule was confirmed in *The Superservant Two* (1990) where one of two barges owned by the defendants and used to transport oil rigs sank. They were, therefore, unable to fulfil their contract to transport an oil-rig belonging to the plaintiff as their other barge (the superservant one) was already allocated to other contracts. The court held that the contract was not frustrated. The plaintiffs had another barge available, but chose not to allocate it to the contract with the plaintiffs. This case illustrates both the court's reluctance to apply the doctrine of frustration and the advantage of using a *force majeure* clause.

- Where the event was foreseeable
  If by reason of special knowledge, the event was foreseeable by one
  party, then the party cannot claim frustration. In *Amalgamated
  Investment & Property Ltd v John Walker & Sons Ltd* (1977) the possibility that a building could be listed was foreseen by the plaintiff
  who had inquired about the matter beforehand. A failure to obtain
  planning permission was also foreseeable and was a normal risk for
  property developers. The contract was, therefore, not frustrated.

The effect of frustration

At common law, the loss lay where it fell, ie the date of the frustrating
event was all important: anything paid or payable before that date
would have to be paid. Anything payable after that date need not be
paid. This rule could be very unfair in its operation, as in *Chandler v
Webster* (1904), where the hirer had to pay all the sum due, despite the
court holding the contract frustrated on account of the cancellation of
the coronation.

In *The Fibrosa Case* (1943) the House of Lords did move away from
this rule and held that where there was a total failure of consideration,
then any money paid or payable in advance would have to be returned.
This rule, however, would only apply in the event of a total failure of
consideration, and could cause hardship if the other party had expend-
ed a considerable amount of money in connection with the contract.

The Law Reform (Frustrated Contracts) Act 1943 was therefore
passed to remedy these deficiencies. It provided:
- s 1(2)
  All sums paid or payable before the frustrating event shall be recoverable or cease to be payable, but the court has a discretionary
  power to allow the payee to set off against the sum so paid expenses incurred before the frustrating event.
- s 1(3)
  Where one party has obtained a valuable benefit before the time of
  discharge, the other party may recover such sums as the court considers just.

Note
These two sections are to be applied independently. The expenses in s
1(2) can only be recovered from 'sums paid or payable before the frustrating event'.

Section 1(3) was applied in *BP (Exploration) Ltd v Hunt* (1982) where
it was held that the court must:

- identify and value the 'benefit obtained';
- assess the 'just sum' which it is proper to award out of the 'benefit obtained'.

The court also stated that:

- the section was designed to prevent unjust enrichment, not to apportion the loss, or to place the parties in the position they would be in had the contract been performed, or to restore them to their pre-contract position;
- in assessing the valuable benefit, the section required reference to the end benefit received by a party, not the cost of performance. In assessing the end benefit, the effect of the frustrating event had to be taken into account;
- the cost of performance can be taken into account in assessing the just sum.

In *BP v Hunt*, BP were to carry out the exploration and provide the necessary finance on an oil concession owned by Mr Hunt in Libya. They were also to provide certain 'farm-in' payments in cash and oil. In return, they were to get a half-share in the concession and 5% of their expenditure in reimbursement oil. A large field was discovered and the oil began to flow; then in 1971 the Libyan government nationalised the field.

The valuable benefit to Hunt was the net amount of oil received plus the compensation paid to the Libyan government which amounted to £85,000,000.

The just sum would cover the work done by BP, less the value of the reimbursement oil already received. This was assessed at £34,000,000. Since the valuable benefit exceeded the just sum, BP recovered their expenses in full. The position would have been very different, however, if the field had been nationalised at an earlier stage and no compensation had been paid.

In *Appleby v Myers* (1867) the plaintiff had completed most of the work under a contract to install machinery on the defendant's premises when the premises were destroyed by fire. The plaintiff failed to recover any money under the common law rules. The position would seem to be the same under the Law Reform Act since there was no end benefit. The defendant's work had been destroyed in the fire. Since there was no valuable benefit' then no just sum could be ordered.

Treitel has criticised this interpretation of the Act. He argues that the destruction of the benefit should be relevant not to the valuable benefit but to the just sum. This interpretation would preserve a useful dis-

cretion for the court, and would be consistent with the wording of the Act. Treitel also claims that s 1(3) is shoddily drafted, and does not address itself to reliance losses which do not result in gain, nor does it seek to apportion the losses between the parties.

Revision Notes

Discharge by performance

Performance must exactly match what was promised. In 'entire' contracts, performance must be complete in order to discharge the contract:

Cutter v Powell (1795)
Sumpter v Hedges (1898)
Bolton v Mahadeva (1972)

Payment may be made on a *quantum meruit* basis:
- Where there has been substantial performance:
  Hoenig v Isaacs (1952).
- Where the contract is divisible.
- Where partial performance has been accepted by the promisee in circumstances where he had freedom to accept or reject partial performance:
  Sumpter v Hedges(1898).
- Where the promisee prevents performance:
  Planche v Colbourn (1898).

Time of performance

In equity
Time is not of the essence of the contract, unless –
- The contract makes it so:
  Lombard North Central v Butterworth (1987).
- Reasonable notice is given to make it so:
  Rickards v Oppenheim (1950).
- The content of the contract makes it so.

At common law
Law follows equity. In *Raineri v Miles* (1981) it was held that late performance will not normally entitle the other party to terminate, but he may sue for damages.

Discharge by agreement

Discharge by agreement may be:
- in accordance with a term in the original contract;
- in accordance with a new agreement, which must be supported by consideration in order to be binding.

Discharge as the result of a breach

A contract may be discharged where it is:
- a breach of a condition;
- a fundamental breach of an innominate term;
- a repudiation.

(See Chapter 3 on Classification of Terms.)

Effect of treating the contract as discharged

A contract may be discharged prospectively, but not retrospectively.

Both parties are discharged from the obligation to perform from the date of termination.

An innocent party may also sue for damages, both for losses sustained before and after the breach.

Anticipatory breach

A party may commit an anticipatory breach of contract by:
- Announcing that he is not going to perform:
  Hochster v De La Tour (1853).
- Disabling himself from performing:
  Frost v Knight (1972).

An innocent party may choose not to terminate the contract as in *White & Carter v McGregor* (1962) provided:
- He can do so without the co-operation of the other party:
  Hounslow UDC v Twickenham Garden Developments Ltd (1971).
- He can show a financial interest in keeping the contract alive:
  The Alaskan Trader (1984).

Discharge by frustration

For the distinction between frustration and a common mistake see *Amalgamated Investment & Property Co Ltd v John Walker & Sons Ltd* (1977).

Definition of frustration

Frustration occurs where it is established that due to a subsequent change in circumstances, the contract has become *impossible to perform*, or it has been *deprived of its commercial purpose*.

Note
The test for frustration is whether there has been a radical change in the obligation.

Circumstances in which frustration may occur

- The subject matter of the contract has been destroyed:
  Taylor v Caldwell (1863)
  s 7 SGA 1979
  cf *Blackborn Bobbin & Co v Allen* (1918).
- Death or incapacity of a party to a contract of personal service:
  Condor v The Barron Knights (1966)
  cf *Mount v Oldham Corp* (1973).
  (Note the effect of illness or imprisonment in the case of employment contracts.)
- The contract has become illegal to perform:
  The Fibrosa Case (1943)
  Avery v Bowden (1855).
- The contract is alleged to have lost its commercial purpose, eg by the failure of an event upon which the contract is based:
  Krell v Henry (1903)
  cf *Herne Bay v Hutton* (1903).
- By government interference which strikes at the root of the contract:
  Metropolitan Water Board v Dick Kerr & Co (1918)
  FA Tamplin v Anglo-Mexican (1916).
- By delay:
  The Nema (1982)
  Jackson v Union Marine (1874).
- A lease may be frustrated but only in rare circumstances:
  National Carriers v Panalpina (1981).

Limits to the doctrine of frustration

'Doctrine must be kept within narrow limits'.

It will not be applied:
* On the grounds of inconvenience, increase in expense, loss of profit:
  Davis Contractors Ltd v Fareham UDC (1956)
  Suez Cases.
* Where there is an express provision in the contract covering the intervening event ie a *force majeure* clause.
  But a *force majeure* clause will be interpreted narrowly (*Metropolitan Water Board v Dick Kerr & Co* (1918)). It will not in any case cover trading with an enemy.
* Where the frustration is self-induced:
  Maritime National Fish v Ocean Trawlers (1935)
  The Superservant Two (1990).
* Where the risk was foreseen by one party.

The effect of frustration

Frustration automatically discharges a contract from the date of the frustrating event. Future obligations are discharged but rights and obligations are incurred before the frustrating event remain.

At common law
* The loss lies where it falls; money paid or payable before the frustrating event cannot be recovered, or must be paid. Money due to be paid after the frustrating event need not be paid:
  Chandler v Webster (1904).
* If there was a total failure of consideration, then any money paid could be recovered:
  The *Fibrosa Case* (1943).

By statute

The Law Reform (Frustrated Contracts) Act (1943)
Section 1(2) provides that all sums paid or payable before the frustrating event shall be recoverable or cease to be payable: but the court has a discretion to allow the payee to set off against sums so paid or payable expenses incurred by him for the purposes of the contract.

Section 1(3) provides that where one party has obtained a valuable benefit, the other party may recover from that valuable benefit such sums as the court considers just.

It was held in *BP (Exploration) Ltd v Hunt* (1982) that the 'valuable benefit' is what remains after the frustrating event.

The Act does not apply to:
- charterparties;
- contracts of insurance;
- contracts for the sale of specific goods;
- contracts where the parties have made their own provisions as to what is to happen in the case of frustration.

9 Remedies for breach of contract

Unliquidated damages (ie damages assessed by the court)

The purpose of unliquidated damages is to compensate the plaintiff for loss suffered as a result of a breach. The purpose is not:

- To punish the defendant
  Punitive damages are not awarded for breach of contract.
- To recoup a gain made by the defendant
  Damages are assessed on the loss to the plaintiff, not on the gain made by the defendant, as in *Teacher v Calder* (1899) where the court refused to award the profit made by the defendant as a result of breaching his contact with the plaintiff. This was confirmed in *Surrey CC v Bredero Homes* (1993) where the court refused damages to the council for a breach of the planning regulations as they could not establish any loss, although substantial gains had been made by the defendants.
  If the plaintiff has not suffered a loss, then nominal damages only will be awarded.

Methods of compensating the plaintiff

Fuller and Perdue identified three kinds of interest in the *Harvard Law Review* in 1936. They are:

- The expectation interest ie loss of bargain basis
  This means putting the plaintiff in the position he would have been in had the contract been performed. This is the traditional basis for awarding damages for breach of contract, and is one of the identifying distinctions between contract and tort.
- The reliance interest ie out of pocket basis
  This means putting the plaintiff in the position he or she was in before the contract was made. It is the basis on which damages are awarded in the law of tort.

Damages on a reliance basis, however, to cover wasted expenditure were awarded for breach of contract in *McRae v Commonwealth Disposals Commission* (1951) (see Chapter 7) because the expectation of profit was too difficult and too speculative to establish.

Damages on a reliance basis were also awarded in *Anglia Television Ltd v Reed* (1972) where the leading actor repudiated his contract at the last moment. The plaintiffs were able to recover all their wasted expenditure on the programme, including those incurred before the contract had been signed.

It has now been established that a plaintiff may choose to claim damages on an expectation or reliance basis, unless it can be shown that damages on a reliance basis would place the plaintiff in a better position than he would be in if the contract had been performed, ie he had made a bad bargain; as in *C&P Haulage v Middleton* (1983) where the plaintiff hired a garage for six months on the basis that any improvements would become the property of the landlord. He was ejected in breach of contract, and sued for the cost of the improvements. It was held that expenditure would have been wasted even if the contract had been performed.

It is for the defendant to prove that the plaintiff had made a bad bargain as in *CCC Films (London) Ltd v Impact Quadrant Films Ltd* (1985) where the defendant failed to prove that the plaintiff would not have made a profit from distributing the films had they been delivered in accordance with the contract.

- Restitution ie return of money or property transferred to the defendant

Restitution is only available only where there is a total failure of consideration.

Contributory negligence

It was held in *Vesta v Butcher* (1988) that contributory negligence can only be raised as a defence where the liability in contract is exactly the same as the liability in tort. It is not relevant for a breach of strict contractual duty (*Barclays v Fairclough* (1994)).

Quantification of damages

Where 'loss of bargain' damages are claimed there are two possible methods of quantification.

* Difference in value.
* Cost of cure.

The court will normally adopt the most appropriate.

In *Tito v Waddell* (1977) where the defendants had agreed to return land to its original condition and replant it after they had finished mining, the court awarded damages on a difference in value basis, as it doubted that the plaintiffs intended to replant the land.

Prima facie rules
* Failure to repair (lease) – difference in value.
* Building contracts – cost of cure.
* Sale of goods – difference in value.

Failure to deliver
The Sale of Goods Act 1979 states that damages will represent the difference between the contract price and the market price (*Williams v Agius* (1914) (see also rules on remoteness and mitigation)).

Failure to accept delivery and pay
The Sale of Goods Act 1979 states that damages will again represent the difference between the contract price and the market price.

But note the position where:

* The seller is a dealer in mass produced goods. In *Thompson v Robinson* (1955) the defendant refused to accept and pay for a Vanguard car he had ordered. It was held that the damages represented the loss of profit on one Vanguard car. The plaintiff had sold

one Vanguard car less than he would otherwise have done during the year.

- The mass produced item is in short supply and the number of sales are governed by supply not by demand. Then there is no loss of profit and damages would not be awarded. In *Charter v Sullivan* (1957) the plaintiff had refused to accept a Hillman Minx he had ordered. Demand exceeded supply for such cars and the plaintiff could sell all he had. It was held there was no loss and nominal damages only were awarded.
- The seller is selling second-hand goods, then the damages revert to the difference between the contract price and market price even if the seller is a garage (*Lazenby Garages v Wright* (1976)).

Incidental or consequential losses may be recovered.

Remoteness of damage

Damages cannot be recovered for losses that are too remote. The losses must be 'within the reasonable contemplation' of the parties.

In *Hadley v Baxendale* (1854) a mill was closed because of the delay of a carrier in returning a mill shaft. The court held that the carrier was not liable for damages for the closure of the mill since he was not aware that the absence of a mill shaft would lead to this conclusion.

The following damages were said to be recoverable:

- those arising naturally out of the breach;
- those which because of special knowledge would have been within the contemplation of the parties.

In *Victoria Laundry v Newman Industries* (1949) the rule was restated and based on knowledge. The laundry was able to recover damages for normal loss of profit following a delay in the delivery of a boiler, but not for especially lucrative dyeing contracts that they were offered during this time. Damages were said to be recoverable for losses which were 'reasonably foreseeable' (a phrase also used in tort) either from imputed knowledge or actual knowledge.

In *The Heron* (1969) the House of Lords stated that a higher degree of foreseeability is required in contract than in tort. Damages were awarded to cover losses arising from the late delivery of sugar to Basra. It was foreseeable that the price of sugar in Basra might fluctuate. For a loss to be foreseeable, there must be 'a real danger'/'a serious possibility' or the loss was 'not unlikely'/'liable to result'.

The difference between the tests of remoteness in contract and tort has been criticised, but justified on the ground that a contracting party can protect himself against unusual risks by drawing them to the attention of the other party to the contract.

Application of remoteness rules

Imputed knowledge
Hadley v Baxendale (1854)
Victoria Laundry v Newman Industries (1948)
The Heron (1969)

Actual knowledge
Defendants' knowledge of special circumstances must be precise. This encourages contracting parties to disclose clearly any exceptional losses in advance.

In *Simpson v L & NWR* (1876), the defendant was liable for loss caused to the plaintiff by delivering goods to Newcastle Show Ground the day after the show had finished.

In *Horne v Midland Rly* (1873) the defendants were held not liable for exceptionally high profit lost by the plaintiff through late delivery. They knew that shoes would have to be taken back if not delivered on 3 February, but not that the plaintiff would lose an exceptionally high profit.

Note
The test of remoteness determines entitlement, not quantum. In *Wroth v Tyler* (1974) the defendant was liable for the full difference between the contract price and the market price, although the rise in the market price was exceptional and could not have been foreseen.

In *Parsons (Livestock) Ltd v Uttley Ingham Co Ltd* (1978) the defendants who had supplied inadequately ventilated hoppers for pig food were held liable for the loss of the plaintiff's pigs, even though the disease from which they died was not foreseeable. It was enough that they could have contemplated any illness of the pigs (but cf *Victoria Laundry v Newman Industries* (1948) where the exceptionally profitable dyeing contracts were held too remote).

Lord Denning in this case, argued that so far as physical damage was concerned (not loss of profit), all direct losses should be recoverable, as in tort.

Lord Scarman has also stated that it would be ridiculous if the amount of damages depended on whether an action was framed in contract or tort.

A House of Lords' decision is awaited.

It is sometimes disputed that the decisions since *Hadley v Baxendale* have in any way clarified the rule, eg the use of the phrase 'reasonably foreseeable' led to doubt as to whether it meant the same in contract as in tort; there is an apparent conflict between the decisions in *Victoria Laundry* and and *Parsons*.

Types of loss recognised

- Pecuniary loss.
- Pain and suffering consequent on physical injury.
- Physical inconvenience
  In *Watts v Morrow* (1991) damages were awarded for the physical inconvenience of living in a house whilst repairs were being carried out.
- Damage to commercial reputation
  In *Gibbons v Westminster Bank* (1939) damages for the injury to his reputation were awarded to a trader whose cheque was wrongly dishonoured.
  In *Anglo-Continental Holidays v Typaldos Lines* (1967) a travel agent recovered damages for loss of goodwill from a ship owner who cancelled a cruise at the last moment.
- Distress to plaintiff
  Traditionally, damages for injured feelings were not awarded for breach of contract (see *Addis v Gramophone Co Ltd* (1909)).
  However, in recent years, exceptions were developed to this rule.
  In *Jarvis v Swan Tours* (1973) damages for disappointment were awarded against a tour operator who provided a holiday which did not correspond with its description.
  In *Cox v Phillips Industries Ltd* (1976) damages for anxiety and distress were awarded to an employee who had been demoted but who had not suffered a diminution in salary.
  However, in *Bliss v SE Thames RHA* (1987) where a consultant sued for the distress he had suffered from being wrongly suspended, the court disapproved of *Cox v Phillips* and confirmed that damages for distress were not available for breach of ordinary commercial contracts.
  In *Hayes v Dodd* (1990) the Court of Appeal confirmed that damages for distress are recoverable only in contracts:

(a) to provide pleasure (see *Jarvis v Swan Tours Ltd* (1973));

(b) to prevent distress (see *Heywood v Wellers* (1976)) where solicitors failed to obtain an injunction to prevent molestation).

It has been suggested that damages for distress are particularly appropriate in 'consumer contracts'.

* Distress to third parties
  See Chapter 10.

* Speculative damages
  The fact that damages are difficult to assess will not normally prevent the court from making an assessment.
  In *Chaplin v Hicks* (1911) the plaintiff recovered damages for loss of a chance to take part in a beauty contest.
  But cf *McRae v Commonwealth Disposals Commission* (1951) and *Anglia Television v Reed* (1972).

Methods of limiting damages

* Remoteness rules (losses which the defendant could not foresee).

* Causation rules (losses which the defendant did not cause).
  The breach must have caused the loss as well as having preceded it. The action of a third party may break the chain of causation, if it is not foreseeable.
  In *Lambert v Lewis* (1982) a farmer continued to use a defective coupling after he knew it was broken. It was held that the responsibility for paying damages lay with the farmer, not the manufacturer.
  But, if the intervention was foreseeable, the chain of causation will not be broken.
  In *Stansbie v Troman* (1948) a painter who in breach of contract left a door unlocked, was held liable for the loss of goods taken by thieves, since this was the kind of loss he had undertaken to guard against by locking the doors. (See also *C&P Haulage v Middleton* (1983).)

* Mitigation (losses which could have been avoided)
  The plaintiff has a duty to take reasonable steps to mitigate his loss.
  In *Payzu v Saunders* (1919) a plaintiff failed to recover damages when he had turned down an offer of goods at below market price.
  In *Brace v Calder* (1895) a dismissed employee had failed to mitigate when he turned down an offer of employment from a partner in his previous firm.

The plaintiff need not take 'unreasonable' steps in mitigation. In *Pilkington v Wood* (1953) it was held unreasonable for the plaintiff to take expensive and uncertain legal proceedings to try to mitigate his loss.

The plaintiff should not take unreasonable steps which would increase losses. In *Banco de Portugal v Waterlow* (1932) the court confirmed that damages would not be recoverable for unreasonable actions, but in that case, found that the bank's action in compensating persons who had been passed stolen banknotes was reasonable.

The plaintiff cannot recover damages for losses he has avoided. In *British Westinghouse v Underground Electric Rly* (1912) the plaintiff was supplied with very inefficient turbines by the defendant. The defendants replaced them with turbines which were far more efficient, although he was not under a duty to do so. It was held that the plaintiff had mitigated his loss and no damages were recoverable.

Note

The duty to mitigate does not arise until there has been an actual breach of contract, or an anticipatory breach has been accepted by the other party. (See *White & Carter v McGregor* (1962) Chapter 8.)

Professor Atiyah has pointed out that the duty to mitigate makes 'an enormous dent in the theory that a promisee is entitled to full protection for his expectations'.

The rules of remoteness, and the reluctance of the courts to grant specific performance also derogate from this theory.

Liquidated damages

Parties to a contract may stipulate in the contract that in the event of a breach, the damages shall be a certain sum or calculated in a specified way.

If the sum represents a genuine attempt to pre-estimate the loss, then it will be enforced by the court as liquidated damages, even if it turns out to be inaccurate. In *Cellulose Acetate Silk Co v Widnes Foundry Ltd* (1925) damages were set in the contract at £20 per working week in the event of a delay in performance. There was a delay of 30 weeks and the loss to the plaintiff was £5,850. It was held that the liquidated damages of 30 weeks x £20, ie £600, would be enforced.

Liquidated damages must be distinguished from:
• Exemption clauses limiting liability
These fix the maximum sum recoverable. If the actual loss is less, then only the lesser sum may be recovered. (See Chapter 5.)

- Penalty clauses
  These are not genuine attempts to pre-estimate the loss, but are designed to frighten the other party into performing the contract, or to punish him. The use of the words 'penalty' or 'liquidated damages' is not conclusive. Whether a sum is a penalty or liquidated damages is a matter of construction. In *Dunlop Pneumatic Tyre Co Ltd v New Garage & Motor Co Ltd* (1915) the following guidelines were suggested:
  (a) a penalty – if the sum is extravagant and unconscionable;
  (b) a penalty – if a larger sum is payable on the failure to pay a smaller sum;
  (c) a penalty – if the same sum is payable on major and minor breaches;
  (d) it is no obstacle to the sum being liquidated damages that a precise pre-estimate is almost impossible.

  Penalty clauses will not be enforced by the court. Instead the court will award unliquidated damages.

  The rule against penalties does not apply to:
- Acceleration clauses
  Here, the whole of a debt becomes payable immediately if certain conditions are not observed.
- Deposits
  ie guarantees that contracts will be performed (these must be distinguished from part-payments). It has been argued that this is illogical since a deposit is a penalty paid in advance of a breach.
- Payments on events other than a breach of contract
  In *Alder v Moore* (1961) a footballer was paid £500 when injury terminated his career, and he agreed to return the money if he played football again. It was held that the rules on penalties did not apply. In *Bridge v Campbell Discount Co Ltd* (1962) it was held that the rule against penalties applied to a minimum payment required on a breach of contract, but did not apply to a minimum payment required when the hirer exercised an option to terminate the agreement in accordance with a term in a contract. (It has been pointed out that a person who breaks a contract is therefore in a better position than a person who complies with it.)
- Clauses stipulating that a term is a condition (see *Lombard North Central v Butterworth* (Chapter 3)).

It is therefore possible to avoid the rule against penalties by wording the contract in such a way as to use one of the above four devices.

Equitable remedies

Specific performance

An order of the court directing the defendant to fulfil his obligations under the contract.
Traditionally, specific performance will only be awarded:

- where damages are not an adequate remedy ie where the plaintiff cannot get a satisfactory substitute;
- for the sale of land;
- for antiques, valuable paintings etc, unless bought as an investment, as in *Cohen v Roche* (1927) where the court refused to order specific performance for a contract to buy Heppelthwaite chairs as an investment;
- where goods cannot be obtained elsewhere;
- where damages are difficult to assess eg annuities;
- where there is no alternative remedy available.

In *Beswick v Beswick* (1968) damages were not available since there was no loss to Peter Beswick's estate. The court, therefore, ordered specific performance of the promise to pay an annuity to Peter Beswick's widow.

It has been argued by Professor Treitel that this case extends the range for the order of specific performance which will now be ordered where it is the most appropriate remedy.

All equitable remedies are discretionary

The following will be taken into account:

- Mutuality
  This has both a negative and a positive aspect. It has a negative aspect in that a minor cannot obtain it because it is not available against a minor, and a positive aspect whereby a vendor of land may obtain it although damages would be an adequate remedy, because it is available to a purchaser of land. (But note that in *Price v Strange* (1978) specific performance was granted to a minor who had already performed all her obligations under the contract.)
- Supervision
  The need for constant supervision prevented the appointment of a resident porter being ordered in *Ryan v Mutual Tontine Association* (1893) but in *Posner v Scott-Lewis* (1987) a similar order was made because the terms of the contract were sufficiently precise.

- Impossibility
  Watts v Spence (1976) where land belonged to a third party.
- Hardship
  Patel v Ali (1984) where the defendant would lose the help of supportive neighbours.
- Conduct of the plaintiff
  Shell (UK) Ltd v Lostock Garages (1977) (Chapter 7).
- Vagueness
  Tito v Waddell (1977) above.
- Mistake
  Webster v Cecil (1861) (Chapter 6).

Special problems

Contracts of personal service
These are considered to involve personal relationships and are therefore not thought suitable for an order of specific performance.

However, in two recent cases, such orders were made – *Hill v CA Parsons Ltd* (1972) and *Irani v Southampton AHA* (1985), on the ground that in the very unusual circumstances of those cases, the mutual trust between the employer and employee had not been destroyed

Building contracts
The courts are reluctant to enforce building contracts, the reason being that damages are generally an adequate remedy, the terms are often vague and there are difficulties with supervision.

However, it was held in *Wolverhampton v Emmons* (1901) that provided the terms were clear, the problem of supervision would not be an absolute barrier.

Injunctions

These are orders directing the defendant not to do a certain act.

Types of injunction
- Interlocutory injunction
  This is designed to regulate the position of the parties pending trial.
- Prohibitory injunction
  This is an order commanding the defendant not to do something.
- Mandatory injunction
  This orders the defendant to undo something he or she had agreed not to do.

Injunctions are also discretionary remedies and are subject to constraints similar to orders of specific performance. However, an injunction will be granted to enforce a negative stipulation in a contract of employment, as long as this is not an indirect way of enforcing the contract.

In *Warner Bros v Nelson* (1937) an injunction was granted to stop Bette Davies working for any film company other than the plaintiff. The court believed that she could earn her living otherwise than as an actress, and would not therefore be forced into performing her contract.

In *Page One Records v Britton* (1968) however, an injunction to prevent the 'Troggs' from appointing another manager was refused. The court considered they did not have the experience to operate without a manager, and an injunction would force them to re-employ the plaintiffs.

A comparison of the remedies for misrepresentation and for breach of contract

Setting aside contracts

Breach
Termination or rescission for breach is available only for breaches of conditions, fundamental breaches of innominate terms and repudiations. The contract is discharged from the time of the breach. Discharge is not retrospective. The innocent party can also sue for damages (see Chapter 8).

Misrepresentation
Rescission is available for all misrepresentations, but at discretion of court, and subject to certain bars. A contract must be cancelled prospectively and retrospectively and the parties returned to the position they were in before the contract was entered into (see Chapter 6).

Damages

Breach
Damages are available as of right.
Damages are normally assessed on an expectation basis.
Losses must be within the contemplation of the parties (see above).

Misrepresentation

Damages are available in tort of deceit, negligent statements, and under s 2(1) Misrepresentation Act 1967.

Damages are assessed on a reliance basis.

All losses flowing directly from the misrepresentation will be covered, whether or not foreseeable, in actions in deceit, and under s 2(1) Misrepresentation Act (*Royscot v Rogerson*, see Chapter 6).

Losses must be foreseeable in the tort of negligence.

There is no right to damages for innocent misrepresentation but damages may be awarded in lieu of rescission at the discretion of the court.

Exclusion clauses

Breach

UCTA ss 3, 6 and 7.

Misrepresentation

All clauses must be reasonable.

Revision Notes

Unliquidated damages (ie damages assessed by the court)

The purpose of unliquidated damages is to compensate the plaintiff for the loss he has suffered as a result of a breach.

Methods of compensating the plaintiff

- Expectation ie loss of bargain basis – this is the traditional basis for assessing damages in contract.
- Reliance ie out of pocket basis – this is the normal basis for assessing damages in tort.
  But because 'expectation' damages would be difficult to assess, damages on a reliance basis were awarded for breach of contract in *McRae v Commonwealth Disposals Commission* (1951) and *Anglia Television v Reed* (1972) (cf *Chaplin v Hicks* (1911)).
  A plaintiff may freely chose between expectation and reliance damages, unless he had made a 'bad bargain' in which cases damages on a reliance basis will not be awarded:
  C&P Haulage v Middleton (1983).
  It is for the defendant to prove that the plaintiff had made a bad bargain:
  CCC Films (London) Ltd v Impact Quadrant Films Ltd (1985).
- Restitution ie return of property transferred by the plaintiff. This is available where there has been a total failure of consideration.
- Consequential losses
  These can also be recovered provided they are not too remote.

Contributory negligence

This is only relevant where the liability in contract is identical with the liability in tort:
Vesta v Butcher (1988).

Quantification of damage

The most common basis for quantifying the loss is 'difference in value' rather than 'cost of cure'.

The Sale of Goods Act 1979 provides that where a seller has refused to deliver or a buyer has refused to accept delivery, the measure of damages should be the difference between the contract price and the market price: *Williams v Agius* (1914).

But if the seller is a dealer in mass produced goods, then the damages to him will represent the loss of profit on one sale: *Thompson v Robinson* (1955).

However, if the goods concerned are in short supply, there is no loss: *Charter v Sullivan* (1957).

The damages revert to the difference between the contract price and the market price in the case of second-hand goods, even if sold by a trader:
Lazenby Garages v Wright (1976).

Remoteness of damage

Damages cannot be recovered for losses that are too remote.

In *Hadley v Baxendale* (1854) it was stated the losses must be 'within the reasonable contemplation' of the parties.

In *Victoria Laundry v Newman Industries* (1949) losses were required to be 'reasonably foreseeable' either from 'actual knowledge' or 'imputed knowledge'.

In *Koufos v Czarnikow Ltd (The Heron)* (1969) the words used were 'a real danger; a serious possibility' or the loss was 'not unlikely' or 'liable to result'.

Application of remoteness rules

Imputed knowledge
Hadley v Baxendale (1854)
Victoria Laundry v Newman Industries (1948)
The Heron (1969)
Pilkington v Wood (1953)

Actual knowledge
The actual knowledge must be precise:
Simpson v L&NWR (1876)
Horne v Midland Rly (1873).

Note
The test of remoteness determines entitlement, not quantum:
Wroth v Tyler (1974)
Parsons (Livestock) Ltd v Uttley Ingham Co Ltd (1978).

But these decisions would seem to be in conflict with that in *Victoria Laundry v Newman Industries* (1848) where the court held that the profit lost on some exceptionally lucrative dying contracts was too remote.

Types of loss recognised

- Pecuniary loss.
- Pain and suffering consequent on physical injury.
- Physical inconvenience:
  Watts v Morrow (1991).
- Damage to commercial reputation.
- Distress to plaintiff:
  In *Bliss v SE Thames AHA* (1987) it was held that damages for distress are only available in contracts:
  (a) to provide pleasure:
  Jarvis v Swan Tours Ltd (1973);
  (b) to prevent distress:
  Heywood v Wellers (1976);
- Distress to third parties:
  This was approved by Lord Denning in *Jackson v Horizon Holidays* (1975) but was disapproved by the House of Lords in *Woodar v Wimpey* (1980) (see Chapter 10).

Methods of limiting damages

- Remoteness rules (see above)
- Causation rules
  The breach must have caused the loss as well as having preceded it:
  C&P Haulage v Middleton (1983)
  Lambert v Lewis (1982)
  Stansbie v Troman (1948).

- Mitigation
  The plaintiff has a duty to take reasonable steps to mitigate his loss:
  Payzu v Saunders (1919)
  Brace v Calder (1895)
  British Westinghouse v Underground Electric Rly (1912).
  The plaintiff need not take unreasonable steps:
  Banco de Portugal v Waterlow (1932).
  Where an anticipatory breach has not been accepted, then the duty
  to mitigate does not arise until the time for performance:
  White & Carter v McGregor (1962).
  See Chapter 8.

Liquidated damages

The parties may stipulate that a certain sum must be paid on a breach
of contract.

If the sum represents a genuine pre-estimate, then it will be enforced
by the court as liquidated damages.

If the sum is not genuine, but is an attempt to frighten the other party
into performing, then it is a penalty. A penalty will not be enforced by
court.

For the distinction between the two see *Dunlop Pneumatic Tyre Ltd v
New Garage & Motor Co* (1915).

The rule against penalties does not apply to:
- acceleration clauses;
- deposits;
- money paid otherwise than on a breach of contract;
- clauses declaring a term a condition.

Equitable remedies

Specific performance
An order directing the defendant to carry out the terms of the contract.

Specific performance is a discretionary remedy, and is only available
where damages are not an adequate remedy:
Cohen v Roche (1927)
Beswick v Beswick (1968).

There are special problems with regard to:
- contracts of personal service where specific performance will not be ordered unless it can be shown that mutual trust and confidence still remain:
  Hill v Parsons (1972).
- building contracts, where specific performance will only be ordered if the terms are clear, and there are no problems with regard to supervision.

Injunctions

Similar conditions apply to injunctions as apply to specific performance, except that an injunction will be ordered to enforce a negative covenant in a contract of service, provided this does not amount to an indirect method of enforcing the contract:
Warner Bros v Nelson (1937)
Page One Records v Britton (1968).

10 Privity of contract

ESSENTIALS

You should be familiar with the following areas: ✓

- meaning of privity
- circumstances accepted as falling outside the rule
- attempts to confer benefits on third parties
- attempts to impose obligations on third parties
- critiques of the doctrine

Meaning of privity

The doctrine of privity of contract consists of two distinct rules.

- A person who is not a party to a contract cannot claim the benefit of it although the contract was entered into with the object of benefiting that third party.

In *Tweddle v Atkinson* (1861) the plaintiff had married Mr Guy's daughter. The plaintiff's father and Mr Guy had agreed together that that they would each pay a sum of money to the plaintiff. Mr Guy died before the money was paid and the plaintiff sued his executors. The action was dismissed since the plaintiff was not a party to the contract which was made between the two fathers.

In *Dunlop Pneumatic Tyre Co Ltd v Selfridge* (1915) Dunlop sold tyres to Dew & Co, a wholesaler, and included a term in the contract that Dew would obtain, from any third party to whom they resold the tyres, an undertaking that they would not retail the tyres under the list price. Selfridge gave Dew such an undertaking, but actually resold the tyres under the list price. Dunlop sued Selfridge for damages, but the suit failed on two grounds: (1) Dunlop had not provided any consideration for the promise; the consideration for Selfridge's promise was given by Dew, and only a person who has provided consideration can enforce a promise; (2) Dunlop was not a party to the contract between Selfridge and Dew and only a party to the contract can enforce the contract.

- A third party cannot be subjected to a burden by a contract to which he is not a party.

In *Dunlop v Selfridge* (above) the House of Lords also held that Selfridge could not be bound by the restriction in the contract between Dunlop and Dew since he was not a party to that contract.

Relationship between privity and consideration

It is argued whether the rule that consideration must move from the promisee is the same as, or different from, the rule that only a party to the agreement can sue. Both rules coincide in the vast majority of cases. The two rules, however, are capable of being distinguished. Chitty furnishes an example.

A man might ... promise his daughter to pay £1,000 to any man who married her. A person who married the daughter with knowledge of and in reliance on such a promise might provide consideration for it, but could not sue on it as he was not a party to the contract.

A person can be party to the agreement, but not provide consideration. If, at the request of A, B promises C that he (A) will pay C £50 if C will dig his garden (Bs), A can be said to be party to the agreement, but does not provide consideration. See also *Beswick v Beswick* (1968).

Established exceptions or circumstances falling outside the rule

It has been argued that it is only because English law has provided many ways of evading the doctrine that the doctrine of privity has survived for so long.

Assignment
Rights can be assigned, without the consent of the other party, provided the necessary formalities are followed.

Agency
If an agent enters into an authorised contract with a third party on behalf of his principal, there is a contract between the principal and the third party.

Multipartite agreements

eg *Clarke v Dunraven* (1897) (see Chapter 1).

The Companies Act 1985 provides that the memorandum and articles bind the company and its members as if signed and sealed by each member, and amount to a covenant between each member and every other member.

Collateral contracts

If a collateral contract can be found, a person not party to the principal contract may sue on the collateral contract, eg in *Shanklin Pier Ltd v Detel* (1951) the plaintiffs employed contractors to paint their pier and instructed them to use the defendant's paints. The defendants had told the plaintiff the paint would last 10 years. It lasted three months.

It was held that the plaintiffs could not sue on contract of sale, but they could sue on collateral contract between themselves and the defendants.

In *Andrews v Hopkinson* (1957) it was held that a customer who had entered into a hire purchase agreement with a finance company on the strength of misrepresentations made to him by the dealer, could sue the dealer on a collateral contract between himself and the dealer. (See also Consumer Credit Act 1974.)

Banker's confirmed credit

A seller of goods may require the buyer to open an irrevocable credit with the buyer's bank in the seller's favour, so that the seller can look to the bank for payment. In *Molas v British Lurex Industries* (1958) a bank refused to honour the confirmed credit and was held to be liable, even though in such cases the seller is a stranger to the bank/buyer agreement (*obiter dictum*).

Trusts

Equity developed the concept of a trust as an exception to the rule of privity. A trust is an equitable obligation to hold property on behalf of another. It may be express or implied, and a person may be trustee of physical property, a sum of money or a chose in action eg a debt.

Land law recognises a number of exceptions to the doctrine of privity.

Leases

The benefits and burdens of covenants in leases are transferred to successors in title of the landlord and tenant if the covenants affect the land.

Restrictive covenants

Covenants inserted into a contract of sale of land may bind subsequent purchasers, provided:

- they are negative in nature;
- the subsequent purchaser has notice of the covenants;
- the person claiming the benefit has land capable of benefitting from its enforcement (*Tulk v Moxhay* (1848)).

Section 56 LPA 1925

A person may take an interest in land or other property or the benefits concerning land or other property although he may not be named a party to the conveyance or other instrument.

This provision abolished the rule that no party could take advantage of a covenant in a deed unless a party to that deed.

Statutory exceptions

Price maintenance agreements
A maximum resale price, or where goods have been exempted by the Restrictive Practices Court, the minimum price, may be enforced not only against a contracting party, but also against a third party who acquires the goods with notice of the agreement.

Insurance
Beneficiaries under certain contracts of insurance may claim the benefit of a contract of insurance, even though they are not parties to it, eg a spouse can take the benefit of a contract of life-insurance entered into by the other spouse under the Married Women's Property Act. Third parties may also sue under the Road Traffic Acts.

Negotiable instruments

Section 56 LPA 1925 (see above)

Attempts to confer benefits on a third party

Allowing the third party to sue

Trusts

An attempt was made to extend the use of trusts. Although no formal words are required, an intention to create a trust, not merely an intention to benefit a third party, must exist. This is the principle reason why the application of a trust concept is uncertain.

In *Walfords Case* (1919) under a charter-party, the shipowner promised the charterer to pay a broker a commission. It was held that the charterer was trustee of this promise for the broker, who could thus enforce it against the shipowner.

However, in *Re Schebsman* (1944) a contract between Schebsman and X Ltd, stating that in certain circumstances his wife and daughter should be paid a lump sum, was held not to create a trust. The Court of Appeal was influenced by fact that Schebsman might have wished to vary the agreement which is impossible in a trust.

The trust as a device to outflank privity seems to have been limited by the courts, presumably because (a) the trust was a 'cumbrous fiction' (b) an insistence that intention to create a trust must be affirmatively proved (c) and a concern lest the irrevocable nature of the trust should prevent the contracting parties from changing their minds. In *Vandepitte v Preferred Accident Ins Corp NY* (1933) the Appeal Court stated:

It is not legitimate to import into the contract the idea of a trust when the parties have given no indication that such was their intention.

Section 56 LPA 1925

Lord Denning launched a campaign against privity, and argued that s 56 intended to destroy doctrine altogether. This was finally rejected by the House of Lords in *Beswick v Beswick* (1968); they acknowledged that the wording (see above) was wide enough to support Lord Denning's view, but insisted, nevertheless, that it must be restricted to the law of real property since the purpose of the Act was to consolidate the law relating to real property.

Agency – in connection with exclusion clauses

Agency has been used to allow a third party to take advantage of an exclusion clause in a contract to which he or she was not a party.

The House of Lords refused to allow stevedores to rely on an exclusion clause in a contract between the carriers and the cargo owner in *Scruttons v Midland Silicones* (1962) on the basis that only a party to the contract could claim the benefit of the contract, ie the exclusion clause. The case caused considerable commercial inconvenience as it made it very difficult for an employer to protect his employees and sub-contractors by inserting an exclusion clause in his contracts, even in those cases where such an exclusion clause was justifiable.

However, in *The Eurymedon* (1975) the Privy Council, on similar facts, held that the carriers had negotiated a second contract (a collateral contract) as agents of the stevedores, and the stevedores could claim the benefit of the exclusion clause in this contract.

But in *Southern Water Authority v Carey* (1985) sub-contractors sought to rely on a limitation of liability clause in a main contract. They were held not to be entitled to the benefit of the clause in the absence of evidence that the main contractor had authority from the sub-contractor to negotiate on his behalf at the time the contract was made; this could not be the case where sub-contractors had not been appointed at the time of the main contract.

This limited the usefulness of collateral contracts. However, in *Norwich City Council v Harvey* (1989) the contract between the main contractor and the owner placed the risk of loss or damage by fire on the owner. It was held that this absolved both the main contractor and the sub-contractors from any liability for loss or damage by fire.

Allowing the promisee to enforce the contract on behalf of the third party

Specific performance

In *Beswick v Beswick* (1968) Peter Beswick had transferred his business to his nephew, in return for his nephew's promise to pay his uncle a pension, and after his death, an annuity to his widow. The nephew paid his uncle the pension, but only one payment of the annuity was made. The widow as administratrix of her husband's estate, successfully sued her nephew for specific performance of the contract to pay the annuity, although the House of Lords implied that she would not have succeeded if she had been suing in her own right.

Thus, if specific performance of a contract can be ordered, a party to a contract or their personal representative can ensure enforcement of the contract for the benefit of a third party. However, the courts will not always order specific performance; it is a discretionary remedy.

Injunction or stay of proceedings

Similarly, an injunction may be awarded to restrain a breach of a negative promise on a suit brought by the promisee, eg A promised B not to compete with C.

However, if the breach of promise consists of pursuing a legal claim against a third party, such an action cannot be stayed by injunction, though a stay of proceedings may be ordered:

- if the contract embodied a promise not to sue the third party; and
- the party seeking to stay the proceedings has a sufficient interest in cause of the action.

In *Snelling v Snelling Ltd* (1973) three brothers lent money to a family company and agreed not to reclaim the money for a certain period. A stay of proceedings was granted to one of the brothers to stop another brother from breaking his promise and suing the company for the return of his money.

Damages

Problems arise where the promisee sues for damages. Damages are normally awarded on a compensatory basis, the promisee will often not have suffered any damage himself; the damage will have been suffered by a third party. It was suggested in *Beswick v Beswick* that if the administratrix had sued for damages, only nominal damages would have been awarded because the estate had not suffered any damage.

In *Jackson v Horizon Holidays Ltd* (1975), the plaintiff entered into contract with a holiday firm for a holiday for his family and himself in Ceylon. The holiday was a disaster. The plaintiff recovered damages for £500 for 'mental stress'. On appeal, the court confirmed the amount on the ground that witnessing the distress of his family had increased the plaintiff's own distress. Lord Denning, however, stated that the sum was excessive for the plaintiff's own distress, but upheld the award on the ground that the plaintiff had made the contract on behalf of himself and his wife and children, and that he could recover in respect of their loss as well as his own.

This statement by Lord Denning was disapproved by the House of Lords in *Woodar Developments Ltd v Wimpey Construction (UK) Ltd* (1980) where the plaintiffs agreed to sell land to the defendants for £850,000. It was also agreed that the defendants should pay part of this amount (£1,500) to a third party. The defendants failed to go ahead with the contract. The plaintiffs sued for damages for breach of contract and asked for damages for the loss to the third party. The House of Lords held that there was no repudiatory breach of contract but went on to discuss the privity issue, and disapproved of Lord Denning's statement in *Jackson v Horizon Holidays*.

Lord Wilberforce, however, did suggest that there was a special category of contracts which called for special treatment where one party contracted for a benefit to be shared equally between a group, eg 'family holidays, ordering meals in restaurants for a party, hiring taxis for a group' and that the decision in *Jackson* could be supported on this ground.

There is as yet, however, no appellate court decision where this suggestion has been applied.

Attempts to impose obligations on a third party

Restrictive covenants

Covenants in a contract for the sale of land may bind subsequent purchasers provided the conditions laid down in *Tulk v Moxhay* apply (see above).

Attempts have been made to extend this rule to personal property. In *The Strathcona* (1926) the plaintiffs had chartered the *Lord Strathcona* for certain months each year. During the period of the charter, the ship was sold to the defendant who refused to allow the plaintiffs to use the ship. The plaintiffs sought an injunction on the ground that the doctrine in *Tulk v Moxhay* should be extended from land to ships. The court granted an injunction.

This decision was criticised in *Port Line Ltd v Ben Line Ltd* (1958) where a ship chartered to the plaintiff was sold to the defendants. The ship was requisitioned during the Suez war and compensation was paid to the defendants. This compensation was claimed by the plaintiffs. It was held that even if *The Strathcona* case was rightly decided, it could not be applied in this case since the defendant was not in breach of any duty and the plaintiff had not sought an injunction but financial compensation which was outside *Tulk v Moxhay*.

The decision in *The Strathcona* has been widely criticised because a contract of hire creates personal, not proprietary rights in the hired object and the retention of land which can benefit from the covenant is a necessary condition of the doctrine in *Tulk v Moxhay*.

Tort of inducing a breach of contract

In *Swiss Bank v Lloyds Bank* (1979) Browne-Wilkinson J considered that the decision in *The Strathcona* was correct. He suggested, however, that the tort of inducing a breach of contract or knowingly interfering with a contract would be a more suitable basis for the decision than *Tulk v Moxhay*, and stated that in his judgment a person proposing to deal with property in such a way as to cause a breach of contract affecting that property will be restrained by injunction from doing so if, when he acquired that property, he had actual knowledge of the contract.

Thus, it would seem that even if the attempt to extend the principle in *Tulk v Moxhay* to chattels has failed, nevertheless, an injunction will be granted in the tort of interfering with or inducing a breach of a contract provided the defendant had actual (as distinct from constructive) knowledge of the existing contract.

The doctrine of privity

Suggested reasons for the doctrine

- Principle of mutuality
  Only a party who can be sued on a contract should be able to sue on it.
- The freedom of parties to vary an agreement would be restricted if third party rights were created.
- Third party beneficiaries are often gratuitous and allowing them to sue would interfere with the doctrine of consideration.

The doctrine has been much criticised; it is said to destroy the legitimate expectations of third parties. It is not found in the law of Scotland or the US. Lord Denning has alleged that it is a 19th century innovation, and has even doubted its existence. He attacked the doctrine in *Scrutton v Midland Silicones; Beswick v Beswick* and *Jackson v Horizon Holidays* (above). But the doctrine was confirmed by the House of Lords in *Beswick v Beswick* and in *Woodar Investment Development Ltd v Wimpey*. However, in *Beswick* Lord Reid stated that if parliament procrastinated further, 'this House might find it necessary to deal with the matter' and in *Woodar* Lord Scarman hoped that if Parliament did not act, that 'this House will reconsider *Tweddle v Atkinson* and other cases which stand guard over this unjust rule'.

In 1991, the Law Commission issued a consultation paper which recommended that third parties should be allowed to enforce agreements made for their benefit, provided the contract indicated an intention to confer an enforceable legal obligation. It also recommended that the third party who sued under this provision would be subjected to any defences available to the promisor against the other contracting party.

The commission also invited comments as to whether acceptance, adoption, or material reliance should be required before the parties are prevented from altering their agreement in a way which affects the third party.

Revision Notes

The doctrine of privity provides that only a party to a contract can sue or be sued on a contract:
Dunlop Pneumatic Tyre Co Ltd v Selfridge (1915)
Tweddle v Atkinson (1861)
Beswick v Beswick (1968).

Circumstances falling outside the rule

Assignment

Rights can be assigned, provided certain formalities are followed.

Agency

A principal can sue and be sued on a contract made by an agent on his behalf.

Trusts

Where a trust has been created, the beneficiary under the trust can sue the trustees even if he was not a party to the original agreement.

Multipartite agreements

In *Clarke v Dunraven* (1897) entrants in a yacht race were allowed to sue each other.

The Companies Act 1985 allows shareholders in a company to sue each other.

Collateral contracts

In limited cases, the court will find a separate (collateral) contract between the promisor and the third party:
Shanklin Pier v Detel Products (1951)
Andrews v Hopkinson (1957)
Land law recognises a number of exceptions.

Leases

The benefits and obligations under a lease can be transferred to third parties.

Restrictive covenants

These can bind a third party under the under the rule in *Tulk v Moxhay* (1848).

Section 56 Law of Property Act 1925

Statutory exceptions

* Price maintenance agreements;
* Various insurance contracts, eg Married Woman's Property Act;
* s 56 Law of Property Act 1925;
* negotiable instruments.

Attempts to confer benefits on a third party

Allowing the third party to sue

Unsuccessful attempts to extend the use of 'trusts':
Walford's Case (1919)
Re Schebsman (1944)
Vandepitte v Preferred Accident Ins Corp (1933).

Unsuccessful attempt by Lord Denning to extend s 56 LPA 1925:
Beswick v Beswick (1968).

Agency was used to allow reliance on an exclusion clause in:
NZ Shipping Co Ltd v AM Satterthwaite & Co Ltd
The Eurymedon (1975)
(cf *Scrutton v Midland Silicones*).

In *Southern Water Authority v Carey* (1985) however, it was held that the negotiator must have specific authority to negotiate on behalf of a second party.

In *Norwich City Council v Harvey* (1989), instead of using an exclusion clause, the contract placed the risk of loss or damage by fire on the owner, and this protected both main contractor and sub-contractor.

Allowing the promisee to sue on behalf of the third party

Specific performance
The promisee may, in appropriate circumstances, obtain an order of specific performance forcing the promisor to fulfil his promise to a third party:
Beswick v Beswick (1968).

Injunction or stay of proceedings
Similarly, the promisee may obtain an injunction or a stay of proceedings against the promisor in order to protect the third party:
Snelling v Snelling (1973).

Damages
Damages to cover the disappointment of a third party was sanctioned by Lord Denning:
Jackson v Horizon Holidays Ltd (1975).

But this was subsequently disapproved by the House of Lords:
Woodar Investment Developments Ltd v Wimpey Construction (UK) Ltd (1980).

Attempts to impose obligations on third parties

Leases

Obligations under a lease may be transferred.

Restrictive covenants

These can be enforced under the rule under the rule in *Tulk v Moxhay* (1848).

The court attempted to extend the rule in *Tulk v Moxhay* to personal property in *The Strathcona* (1926). This approach was criticised in *Port Line v Ben Line* (1958) and in *Bendall v McWhirter* (1952).

The tort of inducing a breach of contract

The decision in *The Strathcona* was approved, however, in *Swiss Bank v Lloyds Bank* (1979) but on the basis that the third party had induced a breach of contract.

Reform of the doctrine of privity

The doctrine has been much criticised, particularly the rule which prevents a third party from enforcing a contract.

* It was attacked by Lord Denning in *Scrutton v Midland Silicones; Beswick v Beswick;* and *Jackson v Horizon Holidays.*
* It is not found in some other legal jurisdictions.
* It destroys the legitimate expectation of the parties.
* It was confirmed by the House of Lords in *Woodar v Wimpey*, but individual members of the House of Lords have recommended reform.
* A discussion paper issued by the Law Commission in 1991 recommended that a third party should be able to enforce a benefit granted to him by contract, provided it was intended to be legally enforceable, and subject to any defences available to the promisor.

Index